Land and the Ruling Class in Hong Kong

Second Edition

Second Edition

Land and the Ruling Class In Hong Kong

by Alice Poon

Enrich Professional Publishing

Published by

Enrich Professional Publishing (S) Private Limited
16L, Enterprise Road,
Singapore 627660
Website: www.enrichprofessional.com
A Member of Enrich Culture Group Limited

Hong Kong Head Office:
1/F., Lemmi Center, 50 Hoi Yuen Road, Kwun Tong, Kowloon, Hong Kong, China

Beijing Office:
Rm 1108A, Culture Plaza, No. 59 Zhongguancun St., Haidian District, Beijing, China

ISBN (Hardback)	978-981-4339-10-0
ISBN (ebook)	978-981-4339-52-1 (pdf)
	978-981-4339-53-8 (epub)
	978-981-4339-54-5 (Kindle)

Enrich Professional Publishing is an independent globally minded publisher focusing on the economic and financial developments that have revolutionized new China. We aim to serve the needs of advanced degree students, researchers, and business professionals who are looking for authoritative, accurate and engaging information on China.

Printed in Hong Kong

Contents

Acknowledgements

I would like to take this opportunity to express my gratitude to Enrich Professional Publishing for bringing this edition to life.

Mention should be made that the inspiration for publishing a Chinese version of this book (co-published by Enrich Publishing and *Hong Kong Economic Journal,* 2010) came from a talk on the first edition of the English title held on April 15, 2010, which was organized by HKReaders, a book store in Hong Kong. I was told by one of the participants that the talk was well received and that many purchase orders for the book were placed after the talk. He said if the book were in Chinese, it would enjoy a much wider readership locally. That was the cue that spurred me into action. I am also indebted to Ronald Yick, the speaker who gave the talk and wrote a review in Chinese.

I must also record my thanks to Canadian Book Review Annual, which selected the first edition as Editor's Choice under the "Scholarly" category for the months of September and October 2007. As a result of that selection, the first edition is now carried in twelve Canadian university libraries, six United States public/university libraries and Cambridge University library (UK). Incidentally, it is also available at Baptist University, University of Hong Kong and Hong Kong University of Science and Technology.

Alice Poon
2010

Abbreviations

APEC	Asia-Pacific Economic Cooperation
CCPI	Composite Consumers' Price Index
COMPAG	Competition Policy Advisory Group
DLO	District Lands Office
EFTNS	External Fixed Telecommunications Network Services
FTNS	Fixed Telecommunications Network Services
GDP	Gross Domestic Product
GEM	Growth Enterprise Market
HKCTU	Hong Kong Confederation of Trade Unions
HKDF	Hong Kong Democratic Foundation
HKEx	Hong Kong Exchanges and Clearing
HKSAR (SAR)	Hong Kong Special Administrative Region
HKT	Hong Kong Telecom
HOS	Home Ownership Scheme
LPG	Liguefied Petroleum Gas
MBOF	Modified Basket of Factors
OFGEM	Office of Gas and Electricity Markets
OFTA	Office of the Telecommunications Authority
PCCW	Pacific Century Cyberworks
PSPS	Private Sector Participation Scheme
REDA	Real Estate Developers Association
RPM	Resale Price Maintenance
SABs	Statutory and Advisory Bodies
SARS	Severe Acute Respiratory Syndrome
SFC	Securities and Futures Commission
UK	United Kingdom
UN	United Nations
UNCTAD	United Nations Conference on Trade and Development
URA	Urban Renewal Authority
US	United States
WKCD	West Kowloon Cultural District

Prologue

*"The reasonable man adapts himself to the world;
the unreasonable one persists in trying to
adapt the world to himself.
Therefore all progress depends on
the unreasonable man."*

- George Bernard Shaw

Since 2005, Hong Kong society seems to have fared steadily worse in terms of her rich-poor gap and social injustice. As this time lapse coincided with Donald Tsang's term of governance, it would perhaps not be unfair to assume that the relentlessly deteriorating situation since he succeeded Tung Chee-hwa as the Chief Executive of Hong Kong must have something to do with the actions or inactions of his administration. Hong Kong people placed high hopes on Tsang when he first came into office, but those hopes have sadly turned into disillusionment.

The chronic unfair social and economic phenomenon, wherein the elite class, with government back-up, exploits unjust land and housing policies and an absence of competition regulations to the detriment of ordinary citizens, has now become deeply ingrained in the social fabric. The objective of the book has been to examine the ultimate and proximate causes of that phenomenon.

The deliberate re-inflating of the property bubble in the last several years by vested interests and its hurtful impact on the everyday life of citizens, in the form of a punishing high living cost environment, further tilted playing field in the economy, and ever shrinking job and business start-up opportunities, has not only drawn ire from the general public, but has particularly incensed the post-80s generation, including the hitherto quiet and tolerant middle class young professionals.

Run-away home prices are only one symptom of an underlying disease that has been plaguing Hong Kong society. Other more pronounced symptoms are: despite Hong Kong boasts of a GDP per capita in 2009 of almost US$43,000, which is on par with Switzerland, she has a high Gini index (rich-poor gap measure) of 43.4, which closely follows Central Africa Republic's 43.6 and is higher than Mainland China's 41.5; she is the third most expensive Asian city to live in;[1] she is the fourth priciest world city to own a home (at US$1,382 a square foot, which is ahead of Tokyo) and she has the second costliest retail space in the whole world.[2] That disease is called "high land price policy", with sickly viruses embedded in the land system and property market structure, which together form the key subject matter of this book.

In 2009, 1.23 million Hong Kongers live below the poverty line. About 100,000 live in squalid cage homes. Li Ka-shing, the Kwok brothers and Lee Shau-kee find themselves standing among the world's top 50 billionaires in the 2009 Forbes List, with respective net worth of US$16.3 billion, US$10.6 billion and US$9 billion. Compared to 2003 net worth figures, their wealth has grown, respectively, by 107%, 59% and 142%. Over this six-year period, the salary index for middle managers and professional employees in Hong Kong has edged up 8.4 percent.[3]

One would need little persuasion to conclude that the age-old schism between the power-wielding property cartel and the masses is continuing to deepen with no end in sight.

Despite the Chief Executive having pledged, on the day of his appointment in June 2005: "to demonstrate to the Hong Kong people that I stand ready to act, and to act in a timely way, for their welfare and interests", the deeply rooted social inequalities and unfairness have steadily worsened under his governance. As a result of government's unpopular actions, apathetic inertia and hesitant half-actions, society has continued to flounder powerlessly in what Premier Wen Jiabao called "a deep-seated conflict".

USURPATION ON PRIVATE PROPERTY RIGHT

The functional constituencies-controlled Legislative Council rammed through a piece of controversial legislation in March 2010, lowering the compulsory sale threshold for 50-year or older buildings from 90 percent to 80 percent amid strong opposition from the general public and democratic legislators. When the Land (Compulsory Sale for Redevelopment) Ordinance was first passed in 1999 with a 90% threshold, the objective was to guard against an impasse wherein one or two owners are untraceable and a developer's acquisition process gets stuck. But this lowering of the threshold is obviously an arbitrary and groundless move that needlessly infringes further on private property right and is slanted blatantly in favor of developers.

In a phone-in radio forum hosted by Carrie Lam, Secretary for Development, a secondary school student asked a hard-hitting question: "Is there any guarantee that the developers won't ask government to further lower the threshold to 70%, 60% or 50%?" Without doubt, the new rule is going to have far-reaching impact on society, especially on the middle class.

As soon as the regulation became effective on April 1, 2010, a developer who had reportedly been negotiating compensation amounts with certain owners (within the remaining 20%) of a 47-year old targeted building in the Mid-Levels backed out from the talks, as the company reckoned it would be worth waiting out till the building turns 50 years old (a wait of 3 more years), when it can then apply for a compulsory sale without the need for haggling with those owners.

Critics of the new rule point out that past records show that almost all the buildings that were the subject of compulsory sale application were located in high-end urban residential districts like the Mid-Levels, which debunks the dubious rationale cited by the Secretary for Development, that the purpose of the law is to facilitate redevelopment of dilapidated areas like Ma Tau Wai.

It has also been discovered that out of a total of 20 cases of compulsory sale that took place since the compulsory sale law was passed in 1999, the buildings in 18 cases were bought by the developer applicants at the reserve price without competition. In a recent compulsory sale case at upscale Braemar Hill, North Point, two blocks of an old residential complex were bought by the New World Group at a ludicrously low price of US$448 per square foot. It can be safely predicted that with the new lower threshold, more flat owners of old buildings situated in upscale areas will be coerced to sell at below market prices even before a compulsory sale is applied for.

If an owner of a targeted building is unwilling to sell, his/her reasons can be twofold: sentimental and practical. On the practical side, the compensation offered by a developer is unlikely adequate for the owner to buy a similar flat in the same neighborhood. If money is not the issue, the preference not to relocate from their long-time nest and a familiar neighborhood, especially for seniors, is only natural and human. Many such unwilling sellers will find they have little recourse when the buildings they live in reach 50 years in age and are targeted by developers.

Under normal land resumption procedures, only government and the Urban Renewal Authority (URA, formerly the Land Development Corporation) have the power to claim back land or property for a public benefit purpose. Since 1999, developers have been handed the same resumption power, but for the purpose of reaping private profits. That power, which shouldn't have been vested in the hands of developers in the first place, has just been given another boost through the lowering of the threshold, and that is what makes the legislation so obnoxious. Legislators seemed to have forgotten that Article 6 of the Basic Law says "The Hong Kong Special Administrative Region shall protect the right of private ownership of property in accordance with the law."

RAIL LINK THAT DERAILS FROM COMMON SENSE

Another piece of highly controversial legislation, bulldozed through Legislative Council by the functional constituency legislators in January 2010, is the approval of the funding of the Guangzhou-Shenzhen-Hong Kong Express Rail Link. The rail link is believed to be the most expensive one on earth and will cost taxpayers US$8.63 billion but will have an estimated return of only US$10.32 billion over 50 years.

The Professional Commons, a group of civically-minded engineers and professionals in other disciplines, had produced a full-fledged alternative rail link proposal which promised to be "faster, cheaper, better" than the government option. The proposal pointed out seven flaws of government's idea of putting the terminal in West Kowloon and argued that a much better location for the terminal would be Kam Sheung Road in the New Territories. Cost-wise, the expert group's proposed link would cost US$3.23 billion, compared to US$8.13 billion under the government option. Moreover, the expert group's proposed rail alignment could eliminate the hassle of having to evict the villagers of Choi Yuen Chuen, who have been putting up a fierce fight with government to protect their homes.

The carefully thought out proposal met with a snide response from officials, who simply refused to budge from their position.

On the day that the funding bill was tabled at a Legislative Council finance committee meeting, thousands of protesters surrounded the Legislative Council building, including twenty post-80s who performed a "prostrating walk" round the building. The protest assembly was largely peaceful, even though at one point some protesters decided to march to Government House to demand a meeting with Donald Tsang, which of course never materialized.

Who stand to benefit most from the construction of the Express Rail Link? Why were the functional constituency legislators so anxious to have the funding bill passed? Perhaps it is because developers' construction subsidiaries and mainland contractors who are well connected to local businesses might be awarded lucrative rail works-related contracts? Perhaps there is more to it.

With the rail terminal being situated adjacent to the West Kowloon Cultural District site, the newly set up West Kowloon Cultural District Authority (WKCD Authority) will probably find good excuses to tender out valuable land parcels within the 40-hectare site for residential or commercial development. Such land tenders, like those conducted by other statutory bodies like the MTR Corporation (MTRC, the company that owns Hong Kong's railways and subways, formerly the Kowloon-Canton Railway Corporation and the Mass Transit Railway Corporation), the Airport Authority and URA, are not subject to Legislative Council oversight. Of course, whether the WKCD Authority will actually tender out land parcels is nothing but pure guesswork on the part of the author. But the guesswork is based on a disbelief that the property cartel could have given up hope on laying their hands on this prime piece of land that is located near what is now a planned transport hub.

UNTENABLE LAND AND HOUSING POLICIES

In terms of apathetic inertia of the Donald Tsang administration, two things that immediately come to mind are: in face of a fast surging property market in the past few years, government has stubbornly refused to resume regularly scheduled public land auction, which has been replaced by an application list system since 2004, after the 2002/2003 moratorium was lifted; and in spite of a public outcry about stratospheric home prices, it has consistently rejected calls to revive the construction of Home Ownership Scheme (HOS)[4] housing, which has been put on hold since 2003.

Residential property prices rose 63% from July 2003 to May 2005, then stalled in the first half of 2006, before marching up another 32.4% between mid-2006 and mid-2008. When the global financial tsunami hit, prices fell 17% between June and December 2008, then rebounded and rose 20% from end-2008 to August 2009. The price surge has since continued unabated and prices have gone up one-third in the last half year.[5]

In October 2009, one developer reportedly sold a luxury flat to a mainland buyer at a price of US$9,197 per square foot. According to the *Wall Street Journal*, mainland buyers account for as much as 40% of new-home sales, thanks to flooding liquidity from the RMB 4-trillion stimulus package put out by the China government in November 2008. There is little doubt that the influx of money from the mainland has contributed to the upward thrust in home prices, in part due to the immigration policy of making property investment as a qualifying option for immigration applicants, the preponderant number of who come from the mainland. While the Australian government, faced with a similar situation there, has already moved to restrict foreign investment in residential properties, the Hong Kong government is still in a sitting duck position.

Reflecting the deep discontent of the post-80s about unaffordable home prices, a popular post-80s blogger who by profession is a medical doctor wrote an open letter to the Chief Executive (published in *Ming Pao*, a daily newspaper) in the same month expressing his views thus:-

"Chief Executive Tsang, do you have any idea how hard it is for the fourth generation to buy a shelter? In the past half year, the prices of a lot of flats have gone up one-third, and rentals have also soared 20 to 30 percent. You tell us we should mind our budget when we consider buying a home. But I want to tell you the young people today are not faring well in terms of home purchase affordability and living expenses. You need to have saved your down payment before buying a home: but most young people are still struggling to repay their university education loans and to pay for further education. Even if you have saved enough for the down payment, you will quickly realize that your budgeted down payment always lag behind the price hikes. For the (newer) properties on which you can take out a 95 percent mortgage, they are all in the HK$2 to HK$3 million (US$258,000 to US$387,000) price range, and these are beyond the purchasing power of a couple with a monthly income of around HK$50,000 (US$6,450). Even if you can consider the less expensive older properties, it would be hard to find a bank who would be willing to do a high percentage mortgage. By the time you have saved HK$100,000 (US$12,900), the price of the target property will have gone up by over HK$300,000 (US$38,700)."

Against a backdrop of what certainly looks like another big bubble in the making, government has preferred to sit tight with arms crossed. At the time of writing this Prologue, government is only planning for two lots to be auctioned but is still undecided on whether or not to resume regular auction (which was a normal practice before the "nine-point plan"[6] was initiated), despite hard evidence of housing supplies falling behind real demand. In the last five years, the average annual flat take-up number has consistently exceeded the net annual increase in new flat supplies. Vacancy rate dropped from 6.8% in 2003 to 4.3% in 2009. Residential rental levels rose 15.4% between the first and fourth quarters in 2009[7] and the steep rise is poised to continue in 2010. In 2008, completed dwellings decreased by 16.1% to 8,800 units, the first time in two decades that the figure is below 10,000.[8]

Executive Council Convenor Leung Chun-ying wrote an article in *Ming Pao* on April 23, 2010 that was a clear rebuttal to the common argument that the 1997/1998 property market crash was caused by Tung Chee-hwa's "85,000 policy".[9] Leung clearly pointed out that when the "Long Term Housing Strategy Review Consultative Document" was publicly announced in January 1997, the Document on which the "85,000 policy" was based, it did not cause the market to tumble then. (The consultation period lasted from January to end of May 1997.) Tung's Policy Address in October 1997 merely announced a policy that emanated from that Document. The author, for one, has always believed that Tung was made a scapegoat when the mainstream media accused him for causing the market to crash with his 85,000 policy.

The main argument that Leung tried to make in the article, with which the author fully concurs, was that government does have a public duty to provide affordable housing for those who need it, in the interests of promoting social stability and a sense of security and sense of belonging among citizens, and that reviving the HOS does not contradict market economy principles.

The 1997 Consultative Document was prepared by Dominic Wong, the then Secretary for Housing, under the then Governor Chris Patten's auspices, in the spirit that dates back to 1976 when the MacLehose administration first introduced the HOS, with the goal of helping all households gain access to adequate and affordable housing and to encourage home ownership in the community. The Document proposes the use of scientific and quantitative models to accurately gauge long-term housing demands, so that it is possible for government to provide sufficient land supplies in a timely manner. It also supports the implementation of subsidized housing schemes to help the middle- and low-income groups to buy their own homes, as well as appropriate measures to dampen speculation in the property market when deemed necessary.

Unfortunately, all those sensible objectives were wiped out in one stroke in 2002 by the nine-point plan. (Readers will find my comments on the nine-point plan in Chapter Four and Chapter Five.) Now government is obviously not inclined to help those who are priced out of the private housing market to own their own shelters through reviving the construction of HOS flats. Even with Legislative Council's passing of a non-binding motion in November 2009 urging government to revive the Scheme, the only response so far is a promise by Tsang to conduct a public consultation on the issue.

When the Housing Society[10] marketed a remaining stock of about 800 "Sandwich Class Housing Scheme" flats in 2010 as a palliative to soothe society's thirst for affordable housing, over 30,000 applications were received, representing an oversubscription of 40 times. Typically, those who want to buy such discounted flats are middle-income earners who have income that exceeds the ceiling set under the HOS but who cannot afford private flats. The discounted flats are subject to a five-year resale restriction which is meant as a deterrent to speculation. The overwhelming response to the sale is a plain indication of the huge demand for affordable housing.

There is one camp in society who believes that government has no duty to give housing aid to the low- to middle-income groups, because it is equivalent to using government subsidies to help these people to profit in the property market, and thus they are opposed to reviving the HOS. To such argument, Leung Chun-ying gives a detailed rejoinder in his May 14, 2010 article in *Ming Pao*. His key point is that government has been in the practice of granting cheap land as subsidies to the industrial and utilities sectors, which has enriched many industrialists and utility company-turned-developers and helped a lot of those involved in such sectors become billionaires. On the other hand, it has never been heard of that a HOS flat owner has profited to such an extent from such government subsidy. Leung questioned why it is not a good thing, in the interests of a bit more even distribution of wealth, if such HOS flat owners are able to profit just a little.

Regarding government's hesitant half-actions, the author cannot think of a more apt example than its recent cooling measures that are targeted at the rule-flouting and unethical sales practices of developers. Most of the measures are nothing but what should have been developers' normal contractual obligations under a fair home purchase and sale transaction involving a substantial amount of consideration, but which have long been high-handedly dismissed by them. Unethical/fraudulent practices like withholding crucial information such as price lists until the last minute, giving misleading information in sales brochures, cheating on the real efficiency ratio of the units, manipulating prices through selectively announcing furtive internal sales, using dribbling sales to increase prices in short intervals, having property agents use pressuring tactics on customers, etc., have been commonplace all these years. Government has been watching silently on the sidelines until now.

However, the so-called cooling measures are so pallid that it is highly questionable whether such cursory measures can effectively dampen speculation and calm the bubbly market, let alone rein in the overpowering developers. The measures are nothing more than just some flimsy guidelines that have no legal binding power. This kind of action looks more like a case of "too little too late". At a June 7, 2006 Legislative Council meeting, Legislator Martin Lee had already proposed a motion to pass legislation to prohibit insider trading, bogus sales, price-rigging and the distribution of false or misleading information, with the aim of enhancing transparency in the property market. The proposal was turned down by Michael Suen, the then Secretary for Housing, Planning and Lands.

In terms of current land and housing policies, the most egregious is Suen's nine-point plan, which reversed all the traditional noble goals of responsible government in this area. The Donald Tsang administration is so held captive by the property cartel that it does not have the gut or gumption to repudiate that plan and revert to practical, socially beneficial land and housing policies based on the 1998 Long Term Housing Strategy White Paper.

Besides, the rationale cited for the nine-point plan that government wanted to stop intervening in the property market was basically a hoax. Being the single largest shareholder of MTRC, it has received dividends of over US$2.58 billion in the past ten years from the company, half of which come from property development profit, as one of its two core businesses is property development. Government has always been a major player in the land and property market and will always be.

Markets, by nature, are subject to incessant fluctuations. Policies based on a publicly declared long term strategy, on the other hand, should be visionary, firm and stable. Market ups and downs should never be allowed to sway set policy goals. Tung made the grave mistake of succumbing to the pressure of property interests when the market tanked, and gave up on sensible long term policy goals in favor of short-sighted, knee-jerk reactionary measures. For fear of upsetting the property cartel, Tsang has been refusing to put an end to Suen's nine-point plan, which should have been a short-term interim measure in the first place. While Tung at least made an initial attempt to take on the cartel, Tsang has loathed doing anything that would rub it the wrong way.

SHORT OF COMPETITION

The cross-sector competition legislation process has been an area where government is seen to be using delaying tactics.

Since government had rejected the Fair Competition Bill proposed by democratic legislators in 2001, the matter was put on the back burner until 2006, when the public was consulted about a cross-sector competition law regime with a full range of regulatory powers and functions. Another round of public consultation on the details of the proposal took place in May 2008.

One key provision of the Competition Bill is that the market share threshold for investigating possible abuse of substantial market power is set at 40%.

Controversial issues about the Bill include: there is no provision in the proposed Bill to control the "abuse of collective dominance", nor any provision that regulates anti-competitive mergers and acquisitions; government, statutory bodies and the utilities sector are proposed to be exempted, although there will possibly be a few exceptions.

Some quarters have estimated the aggregate residential market share held by the top three developers to be 77%. It seems the proposed Competition Bill can do practically nothing about such an obvious anti-competitive situation as it does not seek to deter abuse of collective dominance. Neither will the Bill affect the supermarket industry, where it is known that market shares are highly concentrated in two industry giants. In both cases, unless it can be proven that one of the market share holders has a sole market share of over 40%, it can be safely assumed that the future competition law cannot touch these sectors.

Without any provision to regulate anti-competitive mergers and acquisitions, it means that the property oligarchs are still free to corner any business sector that they have not yet cornered.

As imperfect as the Bill sounds, it is still only a Bill until it is put before Legislative Council for approval. Introduction of the Bill to Legislative Council was postponed once already in March 2009. It was postponed again in July 2009. Other than a statement in a December 2009 speech by Gregory So, Under Secretary for Commerce and Economic Development, that government is "100% committed to introducing the cross-sector competition law, with a target date in the 2009-10 legislative session", nothing much has been heard of lately.

The Scheme of Control[11] Agreements that governs the operation and profitability of the two electricity companies were renewed in 2008 for a term of 10 years, instead of the usual 15. The permitted rate of return is reduced from 13.5-15 per cent to 9.99 per cent. However, as expected, nothing concrete about the opening up of the electricity market has ever been mentioned.

THE MINIMUM WAGE TOIL

After a long uphill struggle by labor unions to push for minimum wage legislation, government finally initiated public debate in 2005. The consultative process had been kept at a snail pace throughout these years until early 2009, when a Provisional Minimum Wage Commission was formed. In 2010, the public discussion focused on the minimum hourly wage rate. Those who detest the Minimum Wage Bill most are naturally those most callous about exploitation of workers, none more exemplary than one functional constituency legislator from the catering industry, who suggested HK$20 (US$2.6) an hour was reasonable. The consultation period ended on May 3, 2010, with the business sector, represented by the Liberal Party, suggesting HK$24 (US$3.1), and various labor organizations calling for HK$30 to HK$35 (US$3.9 to US$4.5).

The figure of HK$35 is arrived at on the basis of a worker having to support himself and one dependant, using a single monthly comprehensive social security assistance payment of HK$2,900 (US$374), times two, plus a transport subsidy of HK$800 (US$103), (i.e. a monthly income of HK$6,600 [US$851]), then divided by six working days a week and eight working hours a day. As at the second quarter of 2009, the median household monthly income was US$2,258.

Legislation of minimum wage has been long overdue in Hong Kong. There is no excuse to delay it for any longer. If Tsang could be said to have done something right for Hong Kong society, it would be the eventual passing of this law with the minimum rate set at least within the range between HK$30 and HK$35 an hour.

A HIJACKED ECONOMY

It may be true that Hong Kong's economy has been recovering from the 2003 nadir, except for the brief dip in 2008 due to the global financial crisis. However, the recovery is perceptible mainly in the form of mainland tourist spending and mainlanders' property investment here. Tourist spending has the effect of boosting retail shop rentals, which mostly benefit the developer conglomerates who own glitzy shopping malls in golden-mile districts, while the money from mainlanders' property purchases goes directly into the pockets of the same people. Those shop rental boosts naturally have a knock-on effect on overall consumer prices, with one feeding the other in a vicious upward spiral.

At the same time, Tsang's economic policy has been focused on "hardware" development, like the building of the Tamar government headquarters, the luxury cruise terminal at the old Kai Tak Airport site, the WKCD and the Express Rail Link, which mainly benefits the property and construction sector.

The economy may have grown as a whole, but little, if any, of the growth goes to benefiting the working class and the grassroots. The so-called "trickle-down effect" that free-market economists believe in can hardly be felt in the real world, as cost-push (especially rental-push) inflation works to erode any hard-to-come-by wage gain.

COLLUSION

Collusion between government and the property cartel has long been a common perception among Hong Kong citizens, but the Leung Chin-man case in 2008 has helped to crystallize that awareness. Leung, former Secretary for Buildings and Lands, had been offered a lucrative employment contract by a New World Development subsidiary after his retirement, but finally gave it up after controversies erupted over his alleged conflict of interest. The job offer was seen by many as equivalent to a "delayed reward" for favors he endowed while holding his official position. How the Civil Service Bureau could even have approved Leung's application to take up the New World Group's job offer in the first place, when it had such a strong appearance of conflict of interest, is just baffling.

Senior officials in departments that deal constantly with the property sector, where colossal amounts of money are involved in daily administrative procedures, naturally face the biggest temptation to succumb to unscrupulous conduct. The more senior the post is and the more executive power the official holds, the higher the tendency is for the profit-driven property cartel to goad that official into a symbiotic relationship.

As revealed in Leung's case, he was allegedly involved in a 2004 decision to sell below market price government's stake in a public-private joint venture project, namely, the Hunghom Peninsula project, which involved two developers: the New World Group and Sun Hung Kai Properties Group. Denise Yue, the Civil Service Bureau chief, admitted that she overlooked Leung's involvement in the project when vetting his application for the New World job.

In another instance in 2005, Leung was criticized by the Audit Commission for having used discretionary power inappropriately over the grant of extra developable gross floor area in the case of Henderson Land's Grand Promenade project, which caused government to lose hundreds of millions in land premium revenue. A subsequent government report claimed that his use of discretionary power was not inappropriate but admitted that the departmental procedures were flawed.

But it seems that government has not learned a lesson from Leung's case, because otherwise it would have actively sought to bring sweeping changes to the current system which does not deter director-grade officials from seeking post-retirement employment that smacks of conflict of interest. The Report from the Committee on Review of Post-Service Outside Work for Directorate Civil Servants is quite toothless (as it seeks to tighten the noose round non-directorate senior staff rather than targeting directorate staff) and was possibly meant as a red herring to distract Legislative Council from digging deeper into the Leung Chin-man case concerning the Hunghom Peninsula project. Government seems to be oblivious of the fact that an honest and scrupulous civil work force is one of Hong Kong's few remaining competitive edges vis a vis rival Mainland cities.

THE POWERFUL SEEKS YET MORE POWER

It is a well known fact that many property tycoons and their close business associates (including many in the banking, legal, architectural, engineering and construction fields), occupy seats on the 800-member Election Committee for the election of the Chief Executive. The property interests are also well represented in the legislature through the real estate and construction functional constituency.

It has been revealed by the *South China Morning Post* that at the end of March 2010, directors of six major property developers held a total of 54 seats on various statutory and advisory bodies (SABs), compared with 16 in 1998. Signs are clear that the property cartel is thrusting its claws deeper into the political system in order to further fortify their economic power.

Their lust for power is often given a prod by government too. David Webb, an independent commentator, made a trenchant comment about the improper lengthy tenure of some of these SABs appointments:-

"The Government has a practice, often honored in the breach, of limiting people to six concurrent appointments and for not more than six years in each seat. In practice it gets around this by re-setting the clock, promoting someone from 'Member' to 'Deputy Chairman' or 'Chairman' of a committee. It regards this as a fresh appointment. Presumably the purpose of the six-year rule is to bring fresh minds and ideas into SABs and also, for those which have economic power, such as the Town Planning Board, to guard against the risk of corruption. It's the same reason why banks move their officers around from branch to branch every few years. It seems inconsistent with both the freshness and anti-corruption objectives to allow someone to progress to the highest position in a committee after six years, where they are even more influential than they were as a member and could preside for another six years."

A six-year term is already inordinately long, not to mention 12 or 18 years. It also seems beyond reason that one person could be allowed to hold as many as six SAB-positions simultaneously, when it is probable that the appointee already holds a full-time job. Perhaps, like Webb says, government is running out of people it trusts to appoint to the SABs, as he has noticed that as soon as these SAB members lose one of their six positions by term expiry, they immediately get appointed to another body. Such power overlap serves nothing but to deepen power concentration in a small elite class and to give a more vivid appearance of government-business collusion.[12]

THE POST-80s AND A PARADIGM SHIFT

Amid an atmosphere of powerlessness that is pervasive in Hong Kong society, a flicker of silver lining in the darkening horizon is becoming visible. The flicker takes the shape of the post-80s' awakening to reality.

A group of Chinese University Student Union members wrote an open letter in June 2009 to all Hong Kong citizens entitled "A Constructive Proposal Dedicated to Our Society's Future", which gives some idea of the cherished ideals of our society's "future hosts".

In a nutshell, the young people of today have a mind-set that is subversively different from that of the older generations who are in possession of great material wealth and hold key positions in the economic hierarchy. Description of their ideals can be epitomized as anti-market fundamentalism, anti-materialism, pro-social justice, pro-humanity, pro-environment and pro-heritage conservation. They also differ from the post-50s in that they are much more outspoken and much less docile and submissive to authority.

The young people's aversion to free market fundamentalism, which centers on a "survival of the fittest" principle and which is much cherished by the post-50 baby boomers, is expressed in this passage in the open letter:-

"It is apparent that this society's rich-poor gap is on equal footing with third world countries, and that cross-generation poverty has brought despair to the young. Such a phenomenon reeks of unspeakable shame. Yet those free market disciples are still running around and declaring: 'The rich-poor gap is an inevitable outcome in economically developed places. There is no need to deal with it, as any responsive action will only impede the overall development of society.' When it is so obvious that text book economic theories run in divergence with the world of reality, the elite class's followers and market believers still use the excuse that 'market will correct itself' to obstruct any policy or measure that is aimed at protecting and caring for the underprivileged."

From the Star Ferry Pier and Queen's Pier social movements to the Wedding Card Street activism,[13] to the more recent Anti-Express Rail Link and Choi Yuen Chuen anti-eviction mass movement, there lies a common key message that the post-80s and other activists spanning all age groups want to send to society: that they are ready to take on the ruling class and are insistent on having a say on how Hong Kong's future should be shaped.

The post-80s are destined to grow into a potent civic force to be reckoned with. Young people are aware of the property oligarchy's monopolizing land and other economic resources and all the unfairness associated with it, and they are determined to fight back. This is one subtle, albeit major, social change that the author had not previously anticipated. It is a welcome and refreshing change indeed.

However, neither the Tung administration nor the Tsang administration has been responsive to the growth in political pluralism and both have been unwilling to engage the public in debate about government policies. Proponents of alternative views have often been dismissed as politically-motivated and obstructionist. While Tung's paternalistic style of governance and emphasis on patriotism riled many Hong Kong citizens, Tsang's stonewalling his opponents and his lack of sensitivity towards the underprivileged is equally irksome for most. But the crux of the matter lies in ruling legitimacy that both administrations sorely lack.

Hong Kong's deep-seated conflicts cannot be properly resolved unless the land and tax systems undergo surgical reform. The systems, after all, are the ultimate spawning ground for class polarization and social injustice. It is improbable, without a democratically elected government, that difficult tasks such as the reforming of the land and tax systems can be successfully tackled.

Chapter 1

The Ruling Class

"In the truest sense,
freedom cannot be bestowed; it must be achieved.""

– Franklin D. Roosevelt

For the 16 consecutive year, Hong Kong was named the world's freest economy by the U.S. based Heritage Foundation in its 2010 Index of Economic Freedom Report. How many would realize, or even admit, that behind all the commendation and applause there is a less-than glorious story to be told. Freedom is a two-edged sword. On the positive side, government's laissez-faire policy has allowed enterprises to grow and flourish in the last few decades, transforming Hong Kong from a modest trading entrepot to the internationally acclaimed financial center it is today. On the other hand, it has also been a catalyst in fomenting an anti-competitive business environment, which has resulted from unchecked industrial and economic concentration and the lack of a comprehensive competition policy, relevant laws and a regulatory body to act as a watchdog and executor of such policy.

There used to be a favorite saying that goes like this: "Hong Kong is controlled, not by the Hong Kong government, but by The Hong Kong Jockey Club and The Hongkong and Shanghai Banking Corporation." That saying is based on the fact that those two organizations are by far the most powerful, in terms of finances, and most influential of enterprises, in terms of their ability to affect people's lives. While there is truth in the first premise, the second one seems arguable in that their influence is only limited to their own patrons (in the case of the Jockey Club, also the charity recipients), rather than all Hong Kong people. So, to say "Hong Kong is controlled" by them seems like an overstatement. Who does wield control over Hong Kong or Hong Kong people, though, is a group of cross-sector corporate giants who, through holding the reins of mainstay economic sectors that lack competition, effectively control or influence both the supply and pricing of certain goods and services that all people in Hong Kong need. Those sectors include property, electricity, gas, public bus/ferry services and supermarket sales.

In most cases, these gigantic corporate entities were initially property developers who had found their first pots of gold in the property sector, and subsequently used their wealth to gobble up money-spinners like utility or public service companies or other conglomerates. The most prominent examples of these cross-sector acquisitions can be found in: (1) Cheung Kong Holdings' acquisition in 1979 of Hutchison Whampoa, a mammoth conglomerate that operates a wide spectrum of businesses, one of which is the Park'N Shop supermarket chain;[1] (2) Sun Hung Kai Properties' gradual control over franchised public bus operator Kowloon Motor Bus (now known as Transport International Holdings Limited), which was initiated in 1980;[2] (3) Accumulation of shares in The Hong Kong and China Gas, the towngas monopoly, by Lee Shau-kee, chairman of Henderson Land, in the period prior to the company's listing in 1981;[3] (4) Hutchison Whampoa's acquisition of Hongkong Electric, one of the two electricity duopolies, in 1985;[4] and (5) New World Development's tendering for and being awarded in 1998 the Hong Kong public bus routes franchise (formerly operated by China Motor Bus) and its acquisition in 2000 of the ferry service licenses from Henderson-controlled Hong Kong Ferry.[5]

CLP Holdings, the other electricity duopoly, has also engaged in cross-sector business activities. Leveraging its earnings from the utility business, the group dabbled in the business of property development in the 1990s. It was as good a case as any of the above where a corporate group gets immensely rich by straddling at least two sectors, both of which are not very competitive. An example of one of its most profitable property ventures is the Hok Un power station site redevelopment in Hung Hom, which was undertaken jointly with leading developer Cheung Kong Holdings.[6]

Another well-known cross-sector conglomerate, the Wharf/Wheelock group, had both its property and public service businesses acquired in a package when the late shipping magnate Y. K. Pao made a successful "come-ashore" bid for the Wharf group in 1980. He gained control, not only of the vast land bank held by the group, but also of its Star Ferry and tram services franchises amongst a variety of businesses. Wheelock Marden, one of the big British "hongs" of the 1970s with property, shipping and retail businesses, became another proud catch of Pao's in 1985.[7] The group subsequently diversified into the telecommunications sector.

Perhaps the most stunning of all utility company acquisitions in Hong Kong's history was Pacific Century Cyberworks' (PCCW) takeover of Hong Kong Telecom (HKT) in August 2000, which was orchestrated by Richard Li, younger son of Cheung Kong Holdings chairman Li Ka-shing.[8] He had earlier made the headlines when, in March 1999, the government announced the granting to PCCW the development right of Cyberport in Pokfulam.[9] This is yet another example of a utility-property hybrid, although, it is claimed, the property portion is used to finance the company's I.T. project.

However, the telecommunications sector is somewhat different from other utilities in that the sector has been undergoing deregulation. HKT had already lost its monopolistic status in 1995 and was subjected to a liberalized operating environment prior to coming under the Li family umbrella. Deregulation of the industry was officially initiated on July 1, 1995 when three newly issued FTNS licenses became effective. Notwithstanding, PCCW is still the industry leader and controls about 80 per cent of the fixed line network market share.[10]

Even with the sector now open to competition, it is still very much an exclusive game for the mega conglomerates, as the three new FTNS licensees are all associated with those conglomerates. They are Hutchison Whampoa's Hutchison Communications, Wharf T & T and New World Development's New World Telephone. These are classic examples of accumulation of utility assets by corporate powerhouses. But some headway has been made in the direction of introducing competition to the industry as competition provisions are written in the FTNS licenses. Also, a watchdog body, the Office of the Telecommunications Authority (OFTA), was set up to act as arbiter on competition matters. From January 2003, the fixed line network industry became fully open to competition and more competitors entered the market. Despite such encouraging development, those operators who are linked to financially strong conglomerates would still be hard to beat as they have sound financial backing from their conglomerate parents and have had first-mover advantage.

In all cases, these property-cum-utility/public services conglomerates are controlled by powerful Hong Kong families: the Lis of the Cheung Kong/Hutchison group, the Kwoks of the Sun Hung Kai Properties group, the Lees of the Henderson group, the Chengs of the New World Development group, the Pao and Woo of the Wharf/Wheelock group and the Kadoories of the CLP Holdings group.

Major listed companies controlled by these economic lynchpins accounted for 14.7 per cent of the total market capitalization (main board) in the Hong Kong stock market by May 2010 (at the end of 2002, the figure was 23.5 per cent - market capitalization has since been diluted by mainland company listings), based on market data compiled by the Hong Kong Exchanges and Clearing (HKEx).[11] Families controlling these companies effectively lord over Hong Kong's key economic sectors and assume virtual rule on Hong Kong people.

As mentioned earlier, Hong Kong's major utility/public service companies, which are considered cash cows as they enjoy monopolistic status, are mostly controlled by property giants with the exception of CLP Holdings, whose controlling shareholder is the Kadoorie family (19.00 per cent).[12] CLP Holdings is the sole supplier of electricity to Kowloon and the New Territories, including Lantau. Hongkong Electric, the sole electricity supplier to the Hong Kong Island, Apleichau and Lamma Island, is 38.87 per cent held by Cheung Kong Infrastructure, which in turn is 84.58 per cent held by Hutchison Whampoa, itself 49.9 per cent owned by Cheung Kong Holdings.[13] The Hong Kong and China Gas is 39.88 per cent held by Henderson Investment and is the sole supplier of towngas in Hong Kong. Henderson Land has a 67.94 per cent interest in Henderson Investment.[14] Transport International Holdings Limited is 33.3 per cent held by Sun Hung Kai Properties and operates the only public bus franchise in Kowloon and the New Territories.[15] First Bus and First Ferry are 100 per cent owned by NWS Transport Services, which is co-owned by NWS Holdings Limited and Chow Tai Fook Enterprises Limited, both are in Chengs' group.[16] First Bus operates one of two public bus franchises on Hong Kong Island while First Ferry operates eight ferry routes under licenses, which it acquired in 2000 from Hong Kong Ferry.

Economists measure concentration in two ways: they gauge the acquisition of assets in industries that are not related, and the control of market share within a sector by a few firms. Both types of concentration are deemed harmful to the economy as a whole. The cross-sector company mergers or asset acquisitions described above are a good proof of the existence of the first type in Hong Kong. As for market share within sectors, specific sectors such as those mentioned above that directly affect the daily lives of the ordinary people show a worrying degree of concentration.

Studies by the Consumer Council in the mid-1990s, initiated under the auspices of the former governor Chris Patten, found that a low level of market competition existed in the market in new residential property and supermarket sales. The Council also recommended a review of statutory monopolies, procedures for awarding franchises and Scheme of Control industries with the aim to introduce competition at the earliest possible opportunity to the utility/public service sector.

A 1996 Consumer Council study revealed that in the period 1991-1994, 70 per cent of total new private housing was supplied by seven developers and that 55 per cent came from just four developers. It also said that one developer consistently supplied 25 per cent of new housing units. The study said: "The market in new residential property in Hong Kong is not highly competitive and not very contestable." It identified some barriers to competition, in particular, the shortage and high cost of land and comparative advantage of those with existing land banks. It went on to say: "It is questionable whether the best interests of consumers have been served under the prevailing market structure in Hong Kong."[17]

Indeed, in the pre-1997 era, developers with the largest land bank were undoubtedly the biggest winners. Even five years after the property market had crashed in 1998 with prices having fallen 65 per cent from the 1997 peak, profits made by the five leading developer conglomerates in the 2002 financial year were still enviable: Cheung Kong Holdings scored US$1.15 billion for the year to December 31, 2002;[18] Sun Hung Kai Properties made US$1.1 billion for the year to June 30, 2002;[19] Henderson Land pocketed US$277 million in the same year;[20] Wharf and Wheelock together collected US$394 million[21] and New World Development made US$168 million.[22] Such phenomenal profits were particularly eye-catching and even ironical, when set against a background of a painfully depressed economy with historically high unemployment. Against the scene of a middle class lying prostrate, victimized by the property market collapse, these developer conglomerates' profit-making ability appeared almost cruelly absurd.

It is no secret that government policies have most of the time favored large developers. One glaring example can be found in government's "nine-point plan" announced in November 2002 aimed at propping up the flaccid property market. The plan focused on reducing the supply of land, including the development land connected with railways, as well as virtually scrapping the long-established subsidized HOS for good. Regardless of government's motive for making the move, the plan was nothing but good news to market-dominant developers, especially those with the largest land banks.

As at June 30, 2009, Sun Hung Kai Properties possessed a land bank comprising 41.9 million square feet of developable gross floor area and 24 million square feet (in site area) of agricultural land.[23] Henderson Land held 19.8 million square feet of developable floor area plus 32.8 million square feet (in site area) of agricultural land as at the same date.[24] In terms of market share, the top three developers supplied 46 per cent of total new private housing stock in the 1991-1994 period, according to the Consumer Council. In 1996, new residential units marketed by these developers accounted for 42 per cent of the total number for that year, according to a survey conducted by leading property agency Centaline. An entrenched market structure characterized by high entry barriers for newcomers, coupled with supportive government policies, will ensure that their dominant market position will be hard to challenge.

The supermarket industry is another sector where competition is least visible. Even without the Consumer Council's issuing its "Report on the Supermarket Industry in Hong Kong" in November 1994, the ordinary Hong Kong resident, from their everyday life experience, would have been able to conclude that the Park'N Shop and Wellcome supermarket chains enjoy a dominant market position. The two supermarket chains together take up 70 per cent of the industry market share, according to the report. The Park'N Shop supermarket chain is owned by conglomerate Hutchison Whampoa and Wellcome is owned by U.K. based Jardine/Hong Kong Land group. Carrefour, the French supermarket chain group, made a brief attempt in the mid-1990s to take on the two giants but soon admitted defeat and left the HKSAR for greener pastures in the mainland. The underlying reason for the French group's retreat is most intriguing and the background story is dealt with in greater depth in Chapter Three.

Towngas in Hong Kong is supplied solely by The Hong Kong and China Gas Company, which operates under a statutory monopoly. Studies by academics have found that in 1997 towngas accounted for 74 per cent of all fuel gas sold and that due to government's laissez-faire policy, The Hong Kong and China Gas Company's profit margin rose from 16 per cent of the average price in the early 1970s to 46 per cent in 1996.[25] In July 1995 Consumer Council issued a report saying that The Hong Kong and China Gas Company's prices and returns were at a level higher than that justified by costs.[26]

Academics and critics have found that CLP Holdings and Hongkong Electric both enjoy duopolistic privileges to the extent that consumers suffer through the lack of industry competition and fair regulatory control. Despite their being governed by a Scheme of Control arrangement, the terms are set in such a way that they provide more of a guarantee to their investment returns rather than a fair regulatory mechanism to guard against abuse of their duopolistic status. Some academics have recommended that, at the expiry of the Scheme of Control arrangement in 2008, structural and regulatory changes to the electricity sector be introduced to enhance competition.[27]

Industrial concentration is honey to the monopoly or oligopoly but venom to the consumer. Consumers have little recourse when they are forced to pay exorbitant prices or rents for a decent shelter, or unjustified high prices for the use of electricity, gas, public bus services or for daily groceries. These are the bare necessities of daily life that one can hardly get by without. Lacking statutory status, the Consumer Council is at best an advisory body that does not even have investigative power. Its function is merely to deal with any complaints filed by consumers and when called upon, conduct studies and prepare reports on controversial issues, and make appropriate recommendations to government. The latter can choose to take action or ignore the Council. Yet this is the only resort Hong Kong consumers can turn to when they are dealt an unfair hand by overbearing conglomerates.

Unbridled, industrial and economic concentration which begets an oligarchy of enterprises would only mean that consumers, for lack of alternatives or bargaining power, are often forced to pay too much for all kinds of basic goods and services. These include a wide range of bare necessities from foodstuffs on supermarket shelves, to gas and electricity, to a bus or ferry ride, to purchasing or renting an apartment. If such concentration were allowed to deepen without restraint, it would cause a crowding out of smaller market players from the marketplace. Evidences show that such a phenomenon is already a common sight. Ever more powerful conglomerates would devour more economic assets, including land, which would lead to more acute concentration of market share in certain sectors and to more cross-sector domination by a single conglomerate. The result: more artificially inflated prices, less product choices, and less bargaining power for consumers. Anti-competitive mergers and acquisitions might also lead to widespread job losses. If allowed to continue without some kind of regulatory control, this predacious game, in which the ruling class assumes more and more economic power and hence more control over the livelihood of the remainder of society, would ultimately dent the economic pie and may even lead to social unrest.

More disturbing is the fact that the families controlling the few corporate empires have a tendency for family perpetuity as regards company ownership and management. This tendency is derived from a deep-rooted Chinese tradition of passing family fortunes from generation to generation. Through the creation of family trusts, which have become a normalcy amongst the rich, the chances of inherited wealth being split by heirs and heiresses going their own separate ways are reduced to a minimum. As such, family-controlled corporate empires in Hong Kong have taken on a life of their own, which may well span several generations. In a capitalist society such as Hong Kong's, accumulation and disposal of wealth at the owner's will is entirely condoned as it concerns an individual's right to private property. That said, perpetuation of family wealth that has been accumulated through abuse of market power made possible by an extremely uncompetitive and unfair operating environment would not be dissimilar to the workings of an antiquated feudal system, where the wealthy assumes power and control over the poor, generation after generation. Such extreme social inequality is quite incompatible with our civilized society and democratic process of today. History tells us that the oppressed would ultimately rise in revolution against the privileged class when polarization between rich and poor reached its extremes. The question is, do we want to be haunted by possible social upheavals, or is there something we can do before it is too late?

In its role as a referee, government has an essential function to perform in balancing the interests of the rich and the less privileged. The least it can do is to heed the Consumer Council's recommendations to set up a competition regulatory body, adopt a comprehensive competition policy and introduce relevant laws. Economically advanced countries have long had competition policy and laws in place. There is no reason why Hong Kong, which has already reached an advanced stage in its economic development, should not follow suit. Indeed, Hong Kong's GDP per capita has reached US$29,826 and ranks about number eleven in the world in 2009. By adopting an effective competition policy, it would be sending out a positive message to the world – that Hong Kong is truly a free economy that encourages competition on a level playing field. To small enterprises and consumers in Hong Kong, it would mean that government genuinely cares about their interests. Regulation in this respect is no antonym to freedom. Rather, it is complementary to the establishment of a more efficient and fair marketplace and would be beneficial to both the economy and society in the long run.

In November 1996 the Consumer Council produced a report entitled "Competition Policy: the Key to Hong Kong's Future Success", which recommended the establishment of a legal framework for a comprehensive competition policy that is consistent across different sectors of the economy. To the public's disappointment, the government only responded nonchalantly by issuing in May 1998 a "Statement on Competition Policy", which merely promised to request government entities to adhere to the Statement and submit new plans on how the promotion of competition could be achieved in their respective sectors. Also, a motion by the Legislative Council on "Anti-monopolization" submitted on January 27, 1999 was rejected by government in February 2001.

Much has been talked about on Hong Kong's comparative advantages versus other mainland cities like Shanghai, Beijing, Guangzhou and Shenzhen, one of them being the freedom of its marketplace. To safeguard that freedom, which all Hong Kong people take pride in, it is crucial to guard against various forms of restrictive practices or behavior and the abuse of market power that artificially inflate prices. Freedom of the marketplace in Hong Kong, which is deemed cornerstone of a capitalistic society and lifestyle, is guaranteed under the Basic Law until 2047. It is the greatest gift bestowed on Hong Kong by the late Chinese leader Deng Xiaoping. In essence, a market is a free market when it has no high entry barriers, where sellers can compete freely with each other on a fair basis, and where buyers do not have to overpay for goods and services and have freedom of choice and bargain. But with the lopsided economic and social structure now prevailing in Hong Kong, this prompts the question of whether she has a genuinely free marketplace.

THE ECONOMIC LORDS

Let us now take a historical and general view of the business empires built up by the giant conglomerates, which are reigned by the most powerful families in Hong Kong.

The Lis

The stable of listed companies under the Li Ka-shing family's control include Cheung Kong Holdings, Hutchison Whampoa, Hongkong Electric, Cheung Kong Infrastructure, CK Life Sciences, Tom.com and PCCW. The combined market capitalization of these companies stood at US$85.3 billion by the end of May 2010. The Cheung Kong group (excluding PCCW) now has businesses in 54 countries, with Cheung Kong Holdings as its flagship. Core businesses of the group include property development, ports and related services, telecommunications, hotels, retail and manufacturing, energy and infrastructure.

Li Ka-shing was born in 1928 in the Province of Guangdong and at the age of eleven migrated to Hong Kong with his parents. His debut enterprise was the manufacture of plastic flowers, from which he earned his first pile of cash. He then set foot in the Hong Kong property market and has become the "lord of lords" in terms of business enterprising, with his empire tentacles spreading over several continents. He fathered two sons, Victor and Richard. Both sons were educated in North America.

Li is the chairman of both Cheung Kong Holdings and Hutchison Whampoa, while elder son Victor is the chairman of Cheung Kong Infrastructure and CK Life Sciences. Younger son Richard is the chairman of PCCW.

With great charisma and a flair for negotiation, Li Ka-shing built up his multi-billion empire by successful deal-making. His milestone feats include the impressive purchase of the majority stake in Hutchison Whampo in 1979 from The Hongkong and Shanghai Banking Corporation, and the well timed acquisition of Hongkong Electric in 1985 from Hongkong Land, when the latter found itself entangled in debt after the property market collapsed in 1983 on the announcement of Hong Kong's sovereignty changeover. Subsequent significant deals include acquisition of Canadian company Husky Oil in 1992 and the 1999 sale of British telecoms company Orange to Germany-based Mannesmann. The latter deal brought him a colossal profit in the region of US$13 billion.

Cheung Kong Holdings has been a leading developer in Hong Kong since the 1960s. The group's more prominent residential projects include Whampoa Gardens (11,224 units in 94 towers), which was built on the old Whampoa dockyard site on the Hung Hom waterfront, Kingswood Villas (15,880 units in 58 towers) in Tin Shui Wai, Yuen Long and Laguna City (8,072 units in 38 towers) in Kwun Tong. As at December 2009 Cheung Kong Holdings held a developable land bank that would be sufficient to support development for the next five or six years. More than 20 years ago the group had already begun to seek out opportunities in other sectors and geographical areas outside Hong Kong and has since become an established international conglomerate.

Richard is said to have taken after his father in being specially gifted in the area of making leviathan and profitable deals. At the age of 27, he became a media star when he concluded the sale of Star TV to media guru Rupert Murdoch of the News Corp group, which took place in July 1993 aboard Murdoch's luxury yacht moored in a Mediterranean port. He used profits from the sale, to the tune of US$390 million, to set up his own company in the same year – the Pacific Century Group, which became listed in Singapore in 1994 via using a shell company.

Far from satisfied with his one-off lucrative deal, Richard had ambitious plans for his newly set up company. Using his connections in the high tech industry in California, he formed Pacific Convergence Corporation with U.S. chip giant Intel in 1998 to invest in information technology research. In 1999, through the backing of the Hong Kong government, the Pacific Century group undertook the development of the US$1.7 billion Cyberport in Pokfulam. In a series of organizational procedures, a Hong Kong listed vehicle was formed in 1999 using the shell company Tricom, which was renamed Pacific Century Cyberworks. This was followed by a series of fund raising activities and acquisitions, which culminated in the US$28.4 billion merger with HKT in 2000. This deal of the century was reportedly concluded with the blessing of the Chinese central government, who was averse to the idea of letting the company fall into the hands of Singapore Telecom, the other suitor.[28]

To have the ability to accomplish so much at such a tender age, Richard probably deserves as much as his father to be called "superman". But one is tempted to ask: "Would he have been capable of such deeds were he not Li Ka-shing's son?" For argument's sake, surely he would not have had the initial big fat capital for starting his own company if in the first place he didn't have the golden chance to work for Star TV – a business established by his father.

The hi-tech bubble burst right after the PCCW-HKT merger caused PCCW's share to lose almost 95 per cent of its value at one point in the two years following. The real "superman" appeared in a high profile lunch meeting with his junior in distress, seemingly to demonstrate in public his paternal support and to restore shareholders' confidence in PCCW.[29] Still, Richard had to face on his own the horrendous task of reorganization, operation streamlining and debt reduction after the HKT takeover, amidst harsh criticism from an irate audience of PCCW shareholders and employees. As a company leader, Richard would need much more than his father's support to return his own company to fit shape.

Compared to Richard, Victor is certainly much more low profile. This heir apparent of the Cheung Kong empire, though occasionally seen in public, mostly at government land auctions, seems to be more media-shy than his sibling.

The heir apparent is the Deputy Chairman and Managing Director of Cheung Kong Holdings and the Deputy Chairman of Hutchison Whampoa. He also holds the chairmanship of Cheung Kong Infrastructure and CK Life Sciences.

Victor was born in 1964 and holds a masters degree in civil engineering. He was married in 1993 to a Catholic. Often seen at his side at land auctions is his colleague Grace Woo, who is an executive director of Cheung Kong Holdings. Another trusted right-hand man of his is Kam Hing-lam, who is the group managing director of Cheung Kong Infrastructure.

One of the development projects that Victor takes most pride in is the Vancouver 1986 Expo site mixed development. The 82-hectare site was purchased in 1988 for C$500 million via tender and is capable of producing 7,650 residential units, 3 million square feet of commercial space, a 400-room luxury hotel and a 630-berth yacht pier. Marketing of the project, which is owned by a consortium called Concord Pacific Development and was spearheaded by Victor, began in 1990 with the launch of its first phase. It met with an overwhelming response as the June 4 Tiananmen incident in 1989 sparked off an exodus of emigrants to Canada. By 1996, a total of 2,100 units in 16 towers were sold, while a portion of the development right was sold to Singaporean and Taiwanese entities for about C$290 million.[30]

As chairman of Cheung Kong Infrastructure, Victor handled several important power asset purchases in recent years in Australia, making the company and Hongkong Electric the largest electricity distributor in that country.

Li Senior has shown himself to be a magnanimous philanthropist, apart from being an astute businessman and deal-maker. By 2002, he forked out a total of US$606 million in donations since the setting up of the Li Ka-shing Foundation in 1980. It will be up to the second generation, once he steps down from the control tower, to decide how far they wish to go in terms of giving back to society.

The Kwoks

The founder of Sun Hung Kai Properties was Kwok Tak-seng, father of Walter, Thomas and Raymond. He was born in 1911 in Zhongshan,

Guangdong, and passed away in Hong Kong in 1990. The brothers took over the management of the company in that year with Walter as chairman and both Thomas and Raymond as vice chairman and managing director.

Major listed companies under the Kwok family's control include Sun Hung Kai Properties - the flagship, Transport International Holdings and Smartone Communications, which together had a market capitalization of US$36.1 billion at the end of 2009. For three years in a row from 1995 to 1997, net profit of the company topped the HK$10 billion (US$1.29 billion) mark, with a historic peak of HK$14.2 billion (US$1.83 billion) reached in 1997. As at June 2009, Sun Hung Kai Properties held a developable land bank of 41.9 million square feet floor area and an agricultural land bank comprising 24 million square feet of site area.

The late Mr. Kwok started out as a trader in the early 1950s with the setting up of Hung Cheong Company, which had the sole sales agency right for the Japanese brand - YKK - zips. Together with Lee Shau-kee and Fung King-hey, named "the three musketeers", he went into the business of property development in 1958 with the establishment of Eternal Enterprises Company. In 1963 their company was restructured and named Sun Hung Kai Enterprises, with Kwok taking up 40 per cent and the chairmanship and Lee and Fung each holding 30 per cent.

In 1972 the three split their partnership and went separate ways. Kwok set up Sun Hung Kai Properties on July 14, 1972, which obtained a public listing status in the same year. The company is now the largest property developer in Hong Kong.

The late founder was a known workaholic and used to work full day Saturdays and half day Sundays. His three secretaries had to take turns to be on duty on Saturday afternoons and Sunday mornings. They were usually rewarded for their extra time and work with a Sunday dim-sum lunch with their boss and family.

Walter and Thomas were both educated in the U.K., while Raymond received his education first in the U.K., then in the U.S. One after the other, they returned to work in their father's company in the late 1970s. Like themselves in those days, their own kids now have finished or are about to finish schooling overseas and some have returned to begin their training in the company.

Perhaps the most memorable event in Sun Hung Kai Properties' first decade since listing was the attempted acquisition in November 1980 of a controlling stake in Kowloon Motor Bus, a public bus service company with large holdings of developable sites in Kowloon used for bus depot purpose. Although the attempt failed technically at the time, it nevertheless opened up a path that led to the subsequent control of the company. It now has a 33.3 per cent stake in Transport International Holdings. Apart from providing a cheap source of land, the company also offers a stable income source from its lucrative franchised bus operation.

Unlike the Cheung Kong group, expansion of the Sun Hung Kai Properties group in the 1970s and 1980s took a vertical form rather than horizontal. Its focus has always been in the development of properties in Hong Kong, from flatted factories to shopping centers, office towers and residential estates. By the mid-1980s, it had established over 100 subsidiaries and associated companies involved in development-related businesses, including construction, property management, electrical and fire services, architectural services, mechanical engineering, concrete production, cement manufacturing, finance and insurance. It had become what people called a typical "property factory". By the end of 1990, Sun Hung Kai Properties' market capitalization reached US$3.26 billion, compared with US$51.6 million at the time of its listing in 1972.

One of the group's most prominent projects in the 1980s was New Town Plaza in Shatin. It was the first comprehensive development of its kind to be carried out in a new town in the New Territories. Phase One of the project, with a gross floor area of 1 million square feet, was completed in 1984. It was the largest commercial development in Shatin and consisted of a huge shopping mall with anchor department stores, retail shops, mini-cinemas, restaurants and an ice-skating ring. It featured the first computer-controlled music fountain to have ever been built in Hong Kong. Phases Two and Three were completed in 1988 and the early 1990s. The development owed its success to the rapid population growth in the late 1970s and early 1980s and the corresponding need to develop new towns in the non-urban areas. The late Mr. Kwok seemed to have a natural gift for doing the right thing in the right place at the right time.

Since the three brothers came to the helm, the most spectacular deal ever landed by them was the group's successful bid in September 2000 for the Mass Transit Railway Corporation's Airport Railway Kowloon Station Packages Five, Six and Seven. The project consists of a total buildable floor area of 5.4 million square feet, with 2.5 million square feet of Grade-A offices in a 102-storey tower, 1 million square feet of luxury residential and service apartment space, 1 million square feet of hotel space and 0.9 million square feet of shopping area. Land cost alone for this project topped US$955 million – probably the highest lump sum cost the group has ever paid for a single development site. The group also has a 47.5 per cent interest in the Central Station development packages on the same railway line.[31]

Banking on its enormous riches, the group also dabbled in the telecommunications sector under the leadership of the brothers through owning a stake in Smartone Communications, the third largest mobile phone company in Hong Kong. At the end of June 2009 the group had a stake of 64.1 per cent. It also has a controlling interest in Sunevision, an I.T. spin-off which was listed in 2000.[32]

Keeping all eggs in one basket – focusing on the Hong Kong property market - has no doubt served the group and the Kwok family well. The three brothers have done well to keep the ship steady so far by adhering steadfastly to that strategy, which they inherited from the late founder. Overall, their reign has been one of relative ease and prosperity.

The Lees

Lee Shau-kee is the only surviving "musketeer" since the trio (Kwok, Lee and Fung) formed alliance in 1958. Born in 1929 in Shunde, Guangdong, to a middle class family, Lee learned the craft of doing business from his father when he was still a teenager. His father was a gold trader and money exchanger.

He moved to Hong Kong in 1948 and ten years later went into a property development partnership with Kwok and Fung. After the split of the partnership in 1972, Lee established his own company Wing Tai Development, which was listed in the same year. His flagship company, Henderson Land Development, was listed in 1981. In 1988, a reorganization of company assets took place, in which development assets were all placed into Henderson Land, while Wing Tai was renamed Henderson Investment and became the listed vehicle for holding non-property assets like interests in The Hong Kong and China Gas and Hong Kong Ferry.

At the end of May 2010, Henderson Land, Henderson Investment and The Hong Kong and China Gas Company had a combined market capitalization of US$28.6 billion. Lee is the chairman of all three companies. Like Kwok, Lee struck jackpot in the property market when he grabbed the golden opportunity of the 1967 riot to go on a land-buying spree. He also began amassing Letter B's,[33] which were to become precious jewels in the money-spinning game of government land bidding in the 1980s and 1990s.

Lee has two sons and a daughter. Elder son Lee Ka-kit was educated in the U.K. and has been working under his father since 1985. He is the vice chairman of Henderson Land and Henderson Investment, and chairman and president of Henderson China. His chief responsibility is the group's property development operation in the mainland. Younger son Lee Ka-shing was educated in Canada and returned in 1995 to work in the group. Daughter Margaret and her husband Li Ning also hold senior positions within the group.

Extraneous as it was to his peaceful character, Lee risked alienating his long time business associate Li Ka-shing by launching a contentious bid in 1993 for the Miramar Hotel group against a competing consortium formed by Li and Citic Pacific's Larry Yung. Although the two contending bids went into a tie at HK$17 (US$2.19) per share, Lee's offer to purchase the Young family's 34.78 per cent stake was finally accepted. Lee came out as the winner because he promised, as a condition of the purchase, to let the existing management keep its status quo after change of ownership, including the managing directorship for Albert Young. Press reports said that Young Chi-wan's widow made a request for that condition to Lee in a closed-door meeting before the offer acceptance announcement. Young Chi-wan was the late founder of the Miramar Hotel group and late father of Albert. He was also a good friend of Lee's. Sadly, Albert passed away two years after the takeover due to a heart disease.[34]

Henderson Land's niche has been in the small- to medium-size residential flats market. One of its well-known land acquisition strategies is to buy out units one by one in targeted old residential buildings in the urban areas like the Mid-Levels, Causeway Bay, Wanchai, North Point and Quarry Bay. In most cases, the sites on which these old buildings stand have some unrealized development potential (unutilized plot ratio) left that can be released upon redevelopment. Needless to say, patience and time are the prerequisites to such a strategy. At December 2009 Henderson Land had a developable land bank comprising 19.8 million square feet floor area and an agricultural land bank consisting of 32.8 million square feet.

Of the largest developers in Hong Kong, Henderson Land is one of those earliest entrants into the mainland property market. Through its listed vehicle Henderson China, which was listed in 1996 amd then privatized in 2005, the group engaged in property development mainly in Beijing, Shanghai, Guangzhou and the Pearl River Delta. At December 31, 2009, Henderson Land had a land bank of 146.2 million square feet of developable gross floor area in mainland China.[35]

The Chengs

Cheng Yu-tung is the chairman and helmsman of the New World Development group of companies, consisting of NWS Holdings, New World China Land and Mongolia Energy Corporation. New World Development, the flagship, had a market capitalization of US$13.8 billion at May 2010. Core businesses of the group include property, infrastructure, public services and telecommunications. New World Development was listed in 1972.

Henry Cheng, the elder son, is the managing director of New World Development and chairman of New World China Land and NWS Holdings, while younger son Peter is an executive director of the latter two companies.

Born in 1922 in Shunde, Guangdong, Cheng Senior has been involved with Chow Tai Fook Jewelry (his private company) and the jewelry trade since the age of 15. He earned the name "King of Jewelry" in the 1960s, with his company holding over ten diamond import licences, importing

30 per cent of Hong Kong's total diamond imports annually. He was another of those lucky property tycoons who dived into the property market during its 1967-1968 nadir and subsequently surfaced with blocks and blocks of gold.

The New World group's monumental property project was New World Centre in Tsimshatsui East, which cost US$181 million and was built in the 1970s in two phases. Phase 1 consisting of New World Hotel, offices and a shopping center was completed in 1978, while Phase 2 consisting of the Regent Hotel and luxury serviced apartments was finished in 1982.

In the 1980s, the group built the Hong Kong Exhibition and Convention Center and two annexed hotels in a joint venture with the Hong Kong Trade Development Council. The Center, together with New World Harbour View Hotel and Grand Hyatt Hotel, became an important landmark on the Wanchai harbourfront.

In 1986, the group went into a joint venture with HKR International to develop Phase 3 of Discovery Bay on Lantau Island, which had a buildable floor area of 1.1 million square feet. Then it bought the development right of Phases 4 and 5, with 1.4 million and 1.0 million square feet of buildable floor area respectively, for US$32.8 million. By the time these developments were completed in the period from 1990 to 1994, the property market soared to new heights. Both companies became loaded from the property sales.

Much to the surprise of his peers, Cheng announced his retreat from the steering wheel in January 1989 to let Henry take over. Henry was born in Hong Kong in 1946 and since graduation from a Canadian university in 1972, has been working in the group.

While in the driver's seat, Henry made several bold moves, including the attempted hostile takeover of the Wing On group in March 1989 and the acquisition of mid-tariff hotel group Ramada Inn hotel chain, which had over 800 hotel properties world-wide. The former venture ended in failure while the latter landed the group in huge debts. In 1991, his dad had to come out of retirement to give him a helping hand.

Once back in control, Cheng started a series of surgical acts aimed at curing the sickly group, including the sale of precious assets like the luxury apartments at the Hong Kong Exhibition and Convention Center in an effort to lower the group's debt level to a more manageable level. At the same time, he made strategic changes to the company operation, refocusing on the core business of property development. By 1995, the New World group resurfaced as one of the four leading developers in Hong Kong.[36]

However, like most other developers, the group could not escape totally unharmed from the 1997 Asian financial fiasco and the subsequent property market collapse. Its precarious debt position forced it to sell its "crown jewel" Regent Hotel in mid-2002 and to carry out an asset restructuring between the group companies in December 2002.

Of all Hong Kong based developers, New World China Land, which was listed in 1999, is one of the companies with the largest land bank in mainland China, standing at 27.75 million square meters (298.5 million square feet) of developable floor area at June 2009.

The group's diversification into the utilities sector began in 1995. It began its telecommunications business when it was awarded a FTNS licence in July 1995. In 1998 it started operating a franchised public bus service and in 2000 began its licensed ferry services.[37]

Pao and Woo

The Wharf (Holdings), Wheelock and Company and i-Cable Communications had a combined market capitalization of US$21.9 billion as at May 2010. The Wharf/Wheelock group was founded by Y. K. Pao, the late shipping magnate who died in 1991. Both Wharf and Wheelock are now chaired by Peter Woo, Pao's son-in-law. Core businesses of the former include property investment, communications, media and entertainment, and logistics (container terminals), and the latter company is principally an investment holding company and property developer.

Pao's acquisition in 1980 and 1985 of the Wharf group and the Wheelock group respectively marked his drastic and successful change of business strategy – one involving a retreat from the shipping industry which was going downhill in the late 1970s and a landing on "on-shore" assets. By gaining control of the asset-rich Wharf group, he took over some of the most valuable properties and sites in Hong Kong – the vast property holdings in Kowloon Point. Today, those holdings comprise the Ocean City, Ocean Centre, Harbour City, Marco Polo Hotel and The Gateway, all high-class commercial rental properties situated in the prime district of Tsimshatsui with a total gross floor area of 8.29 million square feet. Apart from these crown jewels, Pao also gained control of Star Ferry and the Island tram franchised services, as well as container terminals in Kwai Chung. Another gem in the group's commercial portfolio is Time Square, which has a multi-storey shopping podium and two office towers with a total gross floor area of 2 million square feet, standing in the former tram depot site in Causeway Bay. Pao's subsequent take-over of the Wheelock group gave him possession of more commercial properties and other retail businesses including Lane Crawford.[38][39]

Pao was born in 1918 in Ningbo, Zhejiang. He started his career as a banker in Shanghai and in 1949 moved with his family to Hong Kong. He entered the shipping industry by establishing World-Wide Shipping in 1955, which became a renowned international shipping group by the 1970s. Being a suave and diplomatic businessman, Pao had soon elevated himself to the world stage through his sprawling network of political and business ties. By 1973, the number of ships in his fleet increased to 57, with a tonnage of 9.6 million tonnes, far surpassing that of Greek shipping guru Onassis. But just as things were plain sailing, the Middle East oil crisis struck, which led to a plummet in demand for oil tankers. Pao could see trouble coming for the shipping industry and started to draw up his "come-ashore" plans.

In 1978, Pao bought from Li Ka-shing over 10 million of Wharf shares as the first step in his buy-out plan. Then, with the help of The Hongkong and Shanghai Bank, Pao mounted an aggressive bid for the controlling interest in the Wharf group in 1980 and succeeded. Then in 1985 Pao targeted the old British "hong" Wheelock Marden, which subsequently became another trophy of his.

In 1986 Pao decided to retire due to ill health and let Peter take the helm of the Wharf/Wheelock empire. Peter was born in Shanghai in 1946 and educated in the U.S. He married Pao's second daughter Betty in 1973 and played a key role in helping Pao gain control of the Wharf and Wheelock group. Helmut Sohmen, an Austrian who married Pao's eldest daughter, was put in charge of Pao's shipping business. The remaining two sons-in-law were given the respective responsibility of looking after his business in Japan and his private trust funds.

Woo made his mark on the business scene when he led the group into a new era of television broadcasting. Initially he formed a consortium to bid for a cable-TV license in 1988. Although the consortium was awarded the license, the cooperation ended in failure as some key consortium members decided to pull out because of competition coming from adversary Hutchison group, who obtained a pan-Asian satellite TV license and began operating in November 1990. But that did not discourage Woo at all. On the contrary, he decided to go it alone. Ultimately in June 1993 the Wharf group was awarded a cable pay-TV license and began operating as the first pay-TV broadcaster in October under its subsidiary i-Cable Communications.

In 1992, the group decided to take a piece of the fixed line telecommunications market by bidding for a FTNS license through Wharf New T & T (now Wharf T & T). It was awarded the license, which became effective in July 1995, when the Hong Kong Telecom fixed line monopoly officially ended.[40]

Although a successful and rich entrepreneur in his prime, Woo was far from content with his business endeavors. He stunned the public when he announced in 1997 that he was going to run for the chief executive position in the Hong Kong Special Administrative Region, against popular candidate Tung Chee-hwa. Despite his high profile campaign, he lost out to Tung as expected, as the latter collected 320 votes out of 400 in a landslide victory.

That incident aside, Woo still showed his intense interest in public service. He served as chairman of the Hospital Authority from 1995 to 2000 and had been chairman of the Trade Development Council from 2000 to 2007. He also served as council chairman of the Hong Kong Polytechnic University. For the duration of his public service at the Hospital Authority, he relinquished temporarily his management titles at the Wharf/Wheelock group.

The Kadoories

The CLP group was founded in 1901 by Elly Kadoorie, late father of Lawrence and Horace and late grandfather of the current chairman

Michael Kadoorie. The Kadoorie family is the largest shareholder of both CLP Holdings and the Hong Kong and Shanghai Hotels group, with 19 per cent and 50.49 per cent interest therein respectively. Michael is also chairman of the hotel group. As at May 2010, the two companies had a combined market capitalization of US$19.4 billion.

Lawrence Kadoorie was born in 1899 in Hong Kong and started learning the electricity business at the age of 19 from his father. Like many other entrepreneurs of his generation, he was a workaholic. He worked for 74 years for the company until his retirement in 1992, at the age of 93, when he handed control of his utility empire over to his only son Michael. Being a totally dedicated worker, the late chairman had little time left for anything else except for developing a hobby of collecting jade antiques.

Michael was born in 1941 in Hong Kong and educated in Switzerland and the U.K. He married Betty Tamayo in London at the age of 48 and has a daughter named Natalie Louise, who was born in 1986. While his father delved in the passive hobby of art collection, Michael has developed a passion for a much more action-packed sport – that of helicopter flying. But much like his old man, he too fell in love with the finer things in life, like exquisite trimmings and ambience of luxury hotels. For this reason, he spent much of his earlier career managing the affairs of the Hong Kong and Shanghai Hotels group.

In recent years, the CLP group has gradually evolved from a local electricity monopoly operating under a Scheme of Control arrangement into a diversified group, both geographically and sector-wise, as growth potential at its Scheme of Control operations seems to have plateaued.

In 2000, the group took aggressive expansion steps through the acquisition of an 80 per cent equity interest in the Asia Pacific electricity-generating portfolio owned by UK-based Powergen, and the formation of a joint stock company with Beijing Guohua Electric Power Corporation for the purchase of three power stations located in Beijing, Tianjin and Heibei respectively.

In November 2002, the group announced the buying out of Powergen's remaining interest in the Asia Pacific assets, which resulted in CLP owning 100 per cent of Gujarat Paguthan Energy Corporation of western India (the owner-operator of a 655 MW power station), 92 per cent of Yallourn Energy of Victoria, Australia (the owner-operator of a 1,450 MW power station) and 50 per cent of BLCP Power of Thailand (the developer of a 1,434 MW power project).

In mid-2001, the group was awarded an External Fixed Telecommunications Network Services (EFTNS) license, enabling it to make its debut in the telecoms sector by rolling out its ChinaLink services, connecting Hong Kong and the mainland with a new fibre optic cable route for telecoms and internet transmission.

Apart from enjoying a relatively low-risk, steady-growth operating environment over the last decade, the group also has had a good taste of the sweet property pie in the past few years through the joint redevelopment with Cheung Kong Holdings of the Hok Un power station site in Hung Hom, which project was named Laguna Verde. In the bumper harvest years of 1995, 1998, 2000 and 2001, property windfalls contributed 22.7, 19.0, 19.6 and 20.2 per cent respectively of total earnings for the group.[41]

Laguna Verde is a huge residential estate located on the Hung Hom waterfront and was completed in five phases between 1998 and 2002. The project consists of 4,735 residential units in 25 towers and a 280,000 square feet shopping mall called "Fisherman's Wharf". The majority of the units were sold at an average price of over HK$1,000 (US$516) per square foot.

For a new player like the CLP group to overcome entry barriers in the property development field, which is in effect dominated by a handful of property giants, there are three pre-requisites: (1) a strong balance sheet; (2) possession of a cheap land bank; and (3) project management and marketing expertise. The first was obviously a "no-brainer" for the group; the second did not pose a problem as it owns lots of power station sites, some of which, like Hok Un, were no longer in use; and for the third, it had the help of its joint venture partner Cheung Kong Holdings, who is an industry veteran.

That said, the Kadoorie family is by no means a stranger in the property sector. Through the Hong Kong and Shanghai Hotels group, the family owns the famous Peninsula Hong Kong (100 per cent), The Kowloon Hotel (100 per cent), Peninsula New York (100 per cent), Peninsula Chicago (92.5 per cent), Peninsula Bangkok (90 per cent),

Peninsula Manila (40 per cent), Peninsula Beverly Hills (20 per cent) and The Peninsula Beijing (20 per cent). Apart from hotel properties, the group also owns luxury properties in Hong Kong as long-term investments, including The Repulse Bay complex, the Peak Tower and St. George's Building.[42]

A "PRO-DEVELOPER" GOVERNMENT

Conglomerates under the control of the abovementioned families have a stranglehold on some of Hong Kong's economic arteries, namely, property, utilities, public bus service and food retail. The rise to power of these economic lords owes a lot to a government that adopts a laissez-faire approach where it so suits them and at the same time actively protects their interests.

In general, these groups have all been fattened on owning land – the single most valuable natural resource in Hong Kong. Their unrivalled prosperity is in part a by-product of the 50 hectare-a-year land supply ceiling imposed on the Hong Kong British government by the Sino-British Joint Declaration signed in 1984, which caused property prices to sky-rocket during the 1985-1997 period. This special factor apart, the groups have always had government on their side, whether under British or Chinese sovereignty, as government itself, being the sole supplier of land in Hong Kong, has a vested interest in the property sector through the receipt of revenue from land sales and land premiums on lease modification. This has led some academics to criticize the collusive relationship between government and the developers.

It would be fair to say that Chris Patten's government did perceive trouble coming from a property bubble being formed in 1994. It also reacted by attempting to dampen the flaming hot market with counter-speculation measures. Unfortunately, it then became too embroiled in the constitutional squabble with the Chinese side of the Joint Liaison Group to have time or attention left for the property market. Those measures never had a chance of success as they were implemented with half-hearted care.

In the post-handover era, the SAR government started with a "bang" in the form of a high-profile policy to target housing supply at 85,000 flats a year, with an ambitious target for home ownership to reach 70 per cent by the year 2007 (then chief executive Tung Chee-hwa's first policy address on October 8, 1997). In view of the sky-high property prices that were prevalent in the pre-handover period and the public's complaint about the non-affordability of homes, Tung's policy would have been the right "cure" for the over-heated property market, had the timing of its introduction not overlapped the onslaught of the Asian financial crisis. As things turned out, the "bang" ended in a "whimper" when the property market bubble finally burst in late 1997, triggered by that financial crisis. Since then, all fingers pointed at Tung and he was blamed for everything that was connected with the aftermath of the property carnage, like homeowners being caught in the negative equity trap, rising personal and corporate bankruptcies, high unemployment and a rotting economy.

As much as he could not shirk responsibility for failing to admit poor judgment and making prompt corrections to his declared policy (i.e. for lacking political wisdom), that policy was hardly the real trigger of the bubble burst. The real trigger was soaring interest rates brought on by the Monetary Authority in defense of the dollar peg in late 1997, as global hedge funds launched a simultaneous attack on the Hong Kong dollar currency and the stock market, causing widespread panic and sharp price volatility in financial markets. The mayhem later spread to the over-inflated property market like a contagious disease. Like all other bubbles, this one was destined to meet with its inevitable violent end, regardless of whether Tung came up with his policy or not. The laws of gravity always take hold at the end of all bubble cycles. Tung and his policy were merely a steam-releasing valve for property speculators and owners to vent their anger over hefty losses from the carnage. The true cause for the bubble formation is hidden deeper in the land system and the property market structure.

Since reneging on that policy, government became disoriented amidst growing complaints from disgruntled homeowners who had more than 60 per cent of their properties' value shaved off in many cases over the five to six years following the property market bubble burst. In an effort to save the battered property market, government announced a nine-point plan in November 2002 that placed a stress on curbing future flat supplies, with the professed aim of restoring confidence to the ravaged property market. But alas, that plan paradoxically shattered the last ounce of the public's confidence, as it was considered one that favored the developer conglomerates and was of little help to the besieged middle class. By placing a one-year moratorium on land sales, government did a disservice to smaller property players with small land banks, who, without government's intervention, would have been able to boost their land banks at cheaper costs in the then depressed market. This measure, along with planned railway land supply cuts, abandonment of the subsidized HOS and elimination of anti-speculation rules, definitely won applause from the developer conglomerates.

Stanley Ho, the then President of the Real Estate Developers Association (REDA), commended government that it had taken a step in the right direction by introducing the nine-point plan.[43] The plan at least provided a temporary window for the wealthy developers to unload their inventories and get their cash back. By intervening with an aim to arrest the continuous price slide, all government managed to do was contradict its own promise to bring Hong Kong's prices and rents down to more competitive levels relative to her neighbors in the region. Even worse, government created an irrefutable impression that its act was pro-developers.

Against a backdrop of a less-than-level playing field in the local business arena and of consumers being exploited due to conglomerates exerting control over subsistence-linked markets, the locally born and educated middle class of Hong Kong has been strangely reticent about the growing social injustice and the gaping divide that separates the rich from the poor. People in Hong Kong are dangerously apathetic about such phenomenon, all brought about by the unregulated abuse by a few entrenched mega powerhouses of their dominating market position in economic sectors that affect the everyday lives of Hong Kong society. Oddly, an exception can be found in outspoken corporate governance commentator David Webb, who is of foreign descent and who has been one strong advocate for setting up anti-trust or competition laws to deal with anti-competitive behavior in the marketplace, especially in sectors where there are no statutory licensing and inspection provisions. Unchecked, the conglomerates will be able to use their economic power to influence public policy, advance the interests of their associates and/

or penalize others, undermine the position of rivals and deal with their employees/subordinates in a high-handed manner. Unfortunately, such phenomenon is already very much a deja-vu in Hong Kong.

Adding to the problem is that Hong Kong has a government that is "pro-business" rather than "pro-market", as observed by Webb in his article entitled "Hong Kong Needs a Competition Law". He was right in saying that "Efficient free markets can only be achieved if prompt and predictable intervention occurs when competitive forces have disappeared. Sometimes Adam Smith's invisible hand is simply not there." While commending government for gradually dismantling the banking and telecom cartels, Webb's article pointed out that powerful local tycoons who controlled many other sectors were enjoying a laissez-faire public policy and lashed at the lack of regulation, permitting a system of entrenched cartels, impeding economic efficiency.

In allowing anti-competitive behavior to thrive in the business sector, our society is already witnessing a host of social ills, ranging from workers being laid off as a result of mega corporate mergers, to smaller enterprises being elbowed out due to high rents and fees charged by developer landlords, to consumers being robbed of choices and forced to pay unreasonably high prices for basic necessities, to a polarizing gap between the rich and the poor.

In the absence of any regulatory control over economic and industrial concentration, it is not unlikely that our society will go into reverse gear, backing away from a democratization process and moving towards a system that bears likeness to feudalism in the middle ages. The drastic economic downturn in the period immediately after the property market crash already witnessed the wiping out of almost the entire middle class, many of who were unfortunately hurled back down to the lower social echelon as a result of their wealth evaporating into thin air amidst huge losses in the property and stock markets. When the dust settles, the ruling class of economic lords will remain intact. But many of those who had acquired middle class status in the 1980s and 1990s had to bid farewell to this social group. In stark contrast, four of the six aforementioned powerful families were listed among the world's wealthiest league, based on the *Forbes* magazine's 2003 (when Hong Kong economy was in depression) rankings.

In 2010, Li Ka-shing ranked highest in *Forbes* rankings with an estimated worth of US$21 billion and Lee Shau-kee came in second with US$18.5 billion. The Kwok brothers came in third with US$17 billion. According to the statistics of the HKSAR Government, in the first half of 2009, about 17.9 per cent of Hong Kong citizens, some 1.236 million, were classified as families with low-income or in poverty (family members' income was less than half of the median of all Hong Kong households). As the middle class was being substantially scaled back, it looks like society will witness an abysmal divide between the rich minority and the poor majority, which calls to mind the lord and vassal classes of the feudal ages.

Chapter 2

Land and Power

"Power never takes a back step –
only in the face of more power."

– *Malcolm X*

In the type of society found in western Europe in the tenth, eleventh and twelfth centuries, more generally known as the "feudal regime", land was equivalent to power. Land in the middle ages was a source of all wealth and this wealth brought the landlord power in the form of homage from armed men, who were obligated to help their lord to acquire more wealth and defend it for him. In return for their services and obligations, the landlord provided protection and maintenance for his men, or his "vassals". The maintenance initially took the form of a grant by the lord to his vassal of a piece of real property known as a "fief", upon which the vassal could earn his living. However, this originally reciprocal obligatory relationship later developed into one where the lord could demand, by force and coercion, excessive labor services and dues other than land rent from his vassals while offering little or nothing in return. For the 18th century reformers, feudalism in its most basic and precise sense meant the establishment of seigniorial rule of the privileged few over the subordinate majority.

The title *Feudalism* (1961 & 1964) by F. L. Ganshof discusses in detail the various meanings of the word "feudalism". Ganshof says that during the French Revolution, the word was used as a generic description of the many abuses of power in the "Ancien Regime" (ancient regime). The author reckons that feudalism might be interpreted as a form of society that had certain distinct features. These features included the personal dependent relationship at its extreme between a higher social class (often owning military power) and a subordinate class; a system of graded land rights corresponding to the grades of personal dependence; and a distribution of political authority among a group of landlords who exercised in their own interest powers that were normally possessed by the state.[1]

The first English use of the term "feudal system" first appeared in Adam Smith's *Wealth of Nations* (1776). Smith's interpretation of the term was one related to a system of production whereby workers were forced, by the landlord and the state that backed him, to provide labor services, as opposed to being moved to do so by incentives offered by a free market. In his view, such a system inevitably resulted in grudging effort, low productivity and general misery for all except the very wealthy. "Feudal" thus depicted a society that showed sharp contrasts between rich and poor, a distressed and exploited underclass and an unproductive and unresponsive economy.

Today we live in a much freer and more democratic society than in the feudal period. Class distinction, though still prevalent, is far less intransigent. In medieval Europe, restrictions on mobility imposed on vassals by virtue of their labor obligations meant that the dependent class was bonded to their landlords for life. Restrictions on personal freedom were a way of village life in eleventh- and twelfth-century England. Class mobility was simply non-existent.[2] Now in our society, at least in normal times, it is still quite possible for a member of the working class to transcend his own class, through education and hard work, and move up one rung on the social ladder, where some form of asset or wealth possession would allow him material comfort and relief from the bondage of deprivation.

However, in times of economic hardship, the working or under-privileged class are in not much better condition than the medieval vassals, as they are just as helpless and incapable of breaking out from their social bondage. Worse still, during such times many of those who already moved up to join the middle class earlier are easily thrown back down to where they originally belonged. This is what happened in Hong Kong in the aftermath of the 1997/1998 property market debacle. What is ironical is that the power inherent in land and property was instrumental in further strengthening an already powerful elite group here but at the same time led to the downfall of the newly formed middle class. A new situation has surfaced which seems analogous to the feudal period, marked by acutely uneven distribution of wealth. With the near eradication of wealth from the middle class, the super-rich social class (the "lords"), who derived their financial power mainly from land, has assumed overwhelming influence over the remainder of society.

In the early and central middle ages, the amount of land one controlled had a direct bearing on the amount of power one could wield.

In *Property and Power in the Early Middle Ages* (1995) (edited by Wendy Davies and Paul Fouracre) we discover how seigniorial ("seigneurial") rights and powers were developed into political power in many parts of Europe in central middle ages. Major landlords could demand from all who lived in a given territory regular annual dues and dues relating to specific functions provided by the lords like protecting the harvest. Moreover, physical obligations were imposed on those vassals, like castle guarding duty, goods transportation, ploughing, mowing and threshing.

Development of seigniorial rights in Italy was the process by which power over land was turned into power over its inhabitants. Some landlords extended their powers by demanding services from the local population, whether they lived on the landlord's own property or not. By the turn of the eleventh century, local lords with military power in northern Italy increased traditional dues taken from peasants to oppressive levels. From the eleventh century some landlords in East Francia (which later became known as Germany) exercised powers over peasants who lived on lands outside their personal properties as well as those who lived within, having added political powers to their landlordship. In short, power over property increasingly meant power over the people who belonged to the vassal class. Often, the subservient status of the vassals became hereditary too.[3]

"Villains" or villagers in eleventh- and twelfth-century England fared no better than their counterparts in western Europe, according to R. H. Britnell in *The Commercialisation of English Society* (1993). Britnell tells us that villains made up the majority of the recorded population in 1086 in most regions of England and they were ranked low socially, considered only one echelon higher than slaves. He also describes how those villains suffered from the high-handedness of both Cistercian monks and landlords, who, by the arbitrary exercise of seigniorial authority, could sometimes evict them from the lands they tenanted. A large proportion of villains owed labor services on their lord's land as a form of rent. Some labor services covered a whole village community rather than on a specified piece of property and were carried out as a tribute to the lord, that is, a due in addition to rent.

Labor services were a sign of subordination. Villains' subordination to their lords was compounded by restrictions on their mobility and the life bondage imposed on them. Yet their right to their tenanted property was precarious as they could be expelled from it by the landlord at will, and after a tenant's death, his surviving spouse and children had no automatic right to inherit his land. Many lords even had a right to charge a levy on certain types of transaction on their estates, like sales of livestock and ale by their tenants.[4]

In Hong Kong's capitalistic society of today, land also equals power. Large conglomerates derive financial power through the profitable process of property development and investment, and that power enables them to acquire further economic assets.. In the past, their acquisition targets were cash cows like utility and public services, which served to further enhance their financial power with minimal risks. As these economic sectors are closely tied to the daily needs of the ordinary people, these conglomerates, like the lords of the feudal times, do exercise a kind of power or influence on the working class. Such kind of power or influence, though a shade different from that in the feudal ages, is in effect quite similar in terms of the dependent relationship between the humbler social class (ordinary people) and the lordly class (the large conglomerates).

Ordinary people do depend on the large groups for their living maintenance in the form of shelter, food, transport, gas, electricity and bus services etc. In return for the provision of these daily necessities, ordinary people pay in monetized means rather than in the direct form of labor, having first exchanged their labor (work) for money (salary). In the feudal ages, oppression took the form of imposition on vassals by the lords of excessive labor services and unreasonably high dues and arbitrary taxes. Nowadays, oppression of the ordinary people comes in the manner of their being forced to pay excessively for their daily needs, including housing, without any recourse, due to market dominance by the conglomerates. Such oppression is often goaded by government either via active help or a passive laissez-faire approach. In economic hard times, oppression sometimes means workers are laid off without valid reasons or forced to take unreasonable pay cuts as a result of rich enterprises employing high-handed tactics disguised as retrenchment needs. Oppression also means a pro-conglomerate government often targets the middle and working class either for tax increases or imposition of new taxes.

In mediaeval society, power wielded by the rulers and their collusion with the lords was a catalyst in the creation of an extremely inequitable society. *Property and Power in the Early Middle Ages* gives a good description of the depth of the collusive partnership between lords and rulers in most parts of Europe in that period. However, as the influence of royal authority was often weak, power was often concentrated in the hands of local landlords. Still, rulers or royal authority made their presence felt by their ability to impose fiscal, military or judicial dues on landholdings. In all cases, the losers were always the underclass.

In England, by the end of the tenth century, there was often a tendency to incorporate lordship into the administration. Local landlords often formed the backbone of government and the power of office was partly derived from the economic and social power of the landlord. In other words, there was little difference between public power and private power, the latter being based on property. There were cases of rulers attempting to boost their power by raiding the property of others during those times. In general, rulers would persuade those with private local power (or property) to act as their representatives in the locality.

History shows that medieval rulers tended to side with the powerful lords. Incidentally, governments in Hong Kong, both before and after the handover, have shown the same tendency. The pre-1997 colonial government adopted a high land price policy as it depended on land revenue as an important source of income. It was thus able to implement a simple tax system which could benefit British corporations (through a relatively low profits tax regime). That the colonial government was pro-business, in particular pro-British business, went without saying. A major flaw in that policy, though, is that purchasers of private flats have had to bear the tax burden inherent in high property prices, as developers simply passed the entire land cost onto homebuyers. Land receipts, on the other hand, have been mostly spent on building infrastructure, often in a wasteful way and invariably benefiting the land-rich developers, and on maintaining the civil workforce. Little of that public revenue, if any, goes to benefiting taxpayers direct (especially the middle class).

In the post-1997 era, the SAR government has shown itself also to be blatantly supportive of large business groups, despite its repeated vows that it has the public's interest in mind. One vivid example was the granting of the Cyberport site to Richard Li's PCCW in 1999 without first calling a public tender. Other recent examples of government's pandering to developers' whims and wishes include the aforementioned nine-point plan, the West Kowloon Cultural District (government wanted to award the project, which is a 40-hectare site for cultural/residential/commercial development, to one single bidder, a developer conglomerate, out of three), and the Hung Hom Peninsula Private Sector Participation Scheme housing project incident (government sold low-end empty units back to the project developer, probably well knowing the developer's intention of pulling down the never-occupied low-end buildings in order to build brand new high-end ones).

So, in the sense of rulers colluding with economic lords, today's rulers are little different from those of the feudal ages. The major difference is that Hong Kong today has an educated community who has democratic aspirations and expects government to play the role of a referee. As such, it is expected to apply check and balance to the powerful members of society and to help and protect the weak. It is also expected to see to it that no interest group is given any favoritism or special treatment and no business games are played in an unfair manner. To the disappointment of many, it has failed to deliver on all counts. It has already done much harm to its image by portraying itself as pro-conglomerate and apathetic towards the needy. Public confidence in the administration must be restored with no further delay.

Socialists view a government as the guardian of the natural and social resources of a society, which are the common property of all. Land and other natural resources must be treated fairly for public revenue purposes. However, in Hong Kong, a large portion of the public revenue is spent on the civil service payroll. Another problem is, too much of its most valuable resource - land - has fallen into the hands of too few. Our government seems to have more interest in the revenue it earns from land than any regard for the social repercussions of large groups hoarding this scarce and precious resource. This valuable resource has enriched the few large groups so much that they have practically become the ruling class in Hong Kong. The fall of the middle class, through losing out in the property game, has further fortified the position of the ruling class, pushing Hong Kong towards a social crisis that the administration is still unable to perceive, or refuses to acknowledge. Acute concentration of wealth in the hands of the economic lords has divided society into a wealthy oligarchy and a poor, struggling-for-survival majority. Moreover, the absence of an equitable land tax system ensures that these lords can exploit the valuable resource to their absolute advantage without the need to recycle any derived surplus back to society.

Kris Feder shows us in *A Philosophy for a Fair Society* (1994) that American social reformer Henry George had, a century ago, already laid out his solutions for tackling the problem of uneven distribution of wealth and other social ills besetting industrialized and third worlds. Key to the Georgist paradigm is the concept that land (and other natural resources) in a nation rightfully belong to all its citizens and every one should get a share of the common property through the public collection of land rents for public use by means of land taxation. A land value tax would not only pressure owners to put land to its best use, but would also discourage land hoarding and land speculation. Sufficiently heavy taxation of land values would eliminate the incentive to accumulate land with intent to monopolize, Georgists argue. Since no more land can be produced, its exclusive ownership would create barriers to entry and hence monopoly. George was of the view that land hoarding and speculation not only misallocates land, but also leads to widespread economic instability and should be avoided at all costs.[5]

Fred Harrison puts the blame of the collapse of the 1980s in the industrial West on land speculation. He lends his ardent support, in *The Power in the Land* (1983), to a land value tax system that would shift the burden of taxation from labor and capital to economic rent, which is unearned profit on unimproved land. He argues that this would not only increase consumption, through an increase in net household incomes, and stimulate fresh investment, through an increase in post-tax profits, but also create employment and higher growth rates, while avoiding the inflation-prone policy of deficit financing, as increased consumption and investment would be generated by the private sector, not the government. He maintains that exploitation of the unique power in land and land speculation has been the cause of the periodic booms and busts that have regularly troubled industrial economies of the West over the past 200 years. A fairer distribution of wealth and reduced unemployment could be achieved, in his view, by the introduction of a land value tax system, provided the tax was pitched at a deterrent level. Such a system would remove all possibility of profiting from land hoarding and land trading.[6]

Harrison also cited Anthony Harris, a well-known columnist with London's *Financial Times*, as a fervent supporter of land value tax. Harris wrote that a land tax had always seemed appealing in principle as it would fall exclusively on landowners, and it could not be passed on to consumers. Most importantly, it is a tax that falls on those best capable of paying.

A complete overhaul of the tax system may well be what Hong Kong needs to redress the extreme uneven distribution of wealth and social inequality now prevalent in our society. In particular, serious consideration should be given to the introduction of a land value tax system that could discourage land hoarding and speculation. In hindsight, had there been such a tax in place, the land and property price balloon in Hong Kong in the 1992-1997 period and its subsequent bust could perhaps have been avoided.

Financially powerful conglomerates in Hong Kong are all landowners and developers. For some of them, property development is their core business and for others it is a supplementary business. Without exception, they all prospered immensely from the wildest property craze in the history of Hong Kong's property market, which lasted from 1992 to mid-1997. Even before this irrationally hyper-bullish phase, leading developer conglomerates had scored extremely well in the sector for decades and had for a long time been in an unrivalled position. The 1992-1997 bonanza was just a dollop of sugar icings on the cake for them. They were the earliest entrants in the sector, and, through aggressive land buying at every opportunity offered by market troughs in the past several decades, most notably, during the 1967 riots, the 1973 oil embargo crisis and the 1982-1984 property and banking crisis, built up huge land banks. Adding to their comparative advantage is the annihilation of a few of the medium-sized developers after the property market collapsed in late 1997. The market is, now more than ever before, subject to the domination of a few economic titans.

THE POWER IN LAND

The land system in Hong Kong is one inherited from the colonial government. Government owns the superior title to all land. Sale of government-owned land is by way of leasehold grants, through publicly held auctions or tenders. Public land auctions/tenders are conducted in accordance with pre-set programs and annual land sale programs are made public in February or March each year (the land-sale year starts on April 1). At each auction or invitation to tender, the lot put up for sale goes to the bidder who offers the highest price. Development conditions, including the plot ratio (the multiple of buildable floor area relative to site area) and stipulated land use (whether residential, commercial, industrial or others) are all written in the new land grant (called "Conditions of Sale"). Besides complying with such development conditions, a developer would also have to satisfy zoning requirements under the Town Planning Ordinance.

Apart from yearly held auctions/tenders, land is also available for sale through three public corporations: the URA and MTRC. The URA is responsible for identifying urban sites that are ripe for redevelopment and inviting development proposals for such sites from private developers. It is also empowered to resume dilapidated urban properties for redevelopment and negotiate compensation with property owners. MTRC is a transport organization who is responsible for the construction and operation of railway networks and is granted land by government for such purpose. It has authority to sell development rights to the land they are granted (land adjacent to railway lines or the air rights above railway stations), in order to finance the construction of railway lines.

Tenders for URA and MTRC sites are conducted in a semi-private manner in the sense that although invitations for expression of interest are done publicly, the shortlisting discretion lies entirely with the said organizations, which is very much an internal decision made behind closed doors. In the preliminary selection process, two essential criteria have to be met and these are: firstly, the financial strength of the bidder and secondly, the development track record of the bidder. The successful bidder will have to pay a stipulated land premium to government and will have offered a profit-sharing arrangement acceptable to the organization. These site tenders usually involve very sizable amount of buildable floor areas and huge amounts of land premiums payable, compared to normal government land auctions. In the last two decades, Cheung Kong Holdings and Sun Hung Kai Properties have been the leading developers of such sites.

A third source of land available for development is via the lease modification procedure. A piece of land held under an existing land lease with a certain stipulated use can be developed or redeveloped for another use by applying to the Lands Department for a change of use. Such application is called "lease modification application" and would result in the payment of a land premium to government. This procedure is discussed in greater detail in the two sub-sections that follow.

To understand how land became a wealth-churning machine for the developer conglomerates in the decades preceding the property bubble burst, it might help to look into the history of Hong Kong dating back to the 1940s. At the end of the Second World War, the Hong Kong population had dropped to about 500,000 from 1.6 million before the War. However, shortly after the War ended, people began returning at a rate of 100,000 a month. By 1950, the population figure increased to 2.0 million.

At this time, Hong Kong was developing into a manufacturing center and required a huge amount of labor. Immigrants pouring from mainland China provided just the right answer and Hong Kong absorbed them like a sponge, resulting in big surges in population in the 1950s right through the 1970s. The increase in industrial activities and the immigrant influx created a sharp rise in demand for factory and housing space, which meant a goldmine of development opportunities for people savvy enough to spot it. Property tycoons like Li Ka-shing, Lee Shau-kee, Cheng Yu-tung and the late Kwok Tak-seng all saw the golden chance and each one, in his own set of circumstances, made the same right decision in the same right place at the same right time, by embarking in the early-1960s in a big way on what was to become the most lucrative business in Hong Kong for the following four decades.

In the 1960s, those property veterans started out their property business in the industrial sector by building what was known as "flatted factories", which were in great demand as manufacturing activities flourished. They soon extended their development business to the residential sector as population was growing at a bursting rate, which translated into insatiable demand for housing. As it was customary to pay only 30 per cent deposit on land price, the property business then was considered a highly leveraged business. Indeed, the 1965 bank-run brought several medium-sized developers down as they became drowned in debt. The resulting depression and the ensuing riots of 1967 provided an opportune land-hoarding window for the market survivors, some of whom had grown from strength to strength ever since to become powerful "economic lords" of today.

As population and industrial activity increased, so did the demand for land for both housing and factories. In the 1960s, new industrial areas were established in Tsuen Wan and Kwun Tong, with Tsuen Wan being established as the first new town. A survey in the early 1970s showed that 1.8 million people needed to upgrade their living standards and that industrial land supply was very inadequate compared to demand. As land in urban Hong Kong and Kowloon was becoming scarce by the day, government had to develop three more new towns in the New Territories, that is, Shatin, Tai Po and Tuen Mun. The development program was later expanded to include five more new towns, with an aim to provide housing for about three million inhabitants.[7] These new town developments provided a nest of golden eggs for leading developers Sun Hung Kai Properties and Henderson Land, who were the most aggressive of buyers of agricultural land and land exchange entitlements in the New Territories in the 1970s and 1980s.

Before the 1967 riots, the British "hongs" like Jardines, Hong Kong Land, Wheelock Marden, Swire Pacific and Hutchison had a general stranglehold on Hong Kong's economy and prime urban sites. Their tight control of such was beyond the challenge of most Chinese businessmen or enterprises. But the riots, which were connected with China's infamous Cultural Revolution, caused an irrevocable change to that situation in the ensuing years. In the late 1960s up to the mid-1970s, the British hongs began to scale down investments and dispose of their land and property assets in the face of political turmoil in the mainland brought on by the "Gang of Four". In contrary, the Chinese property entrepreneurs used the market trough of the 1965-1967 period to snap up cheap development sites. In the early-1970s, Chinese companies like Cheung Kong, Sun Hung Kai Properties, Wing Tai (Lee Shau-kee's private company, which was later reorganized into Henderson Investment in the 1980s) and New World Development grasped the opportunity to strengthen their financial position by making well-timed use of the stock market to raise funds through public listing. Funds thus raised were used to increase their landholdings avidly.

Between the end-1970s and mid-1980s, ownership of large land-rich British companies like Hutchison Whampoa, Green Island Cement, Hongkong Electric, Wharf and Wheelock Marden fell into the hands of Chinese tycoons Li Ka-shing and Y. K. Pao. Acquisition of these land-rich companies gave a strong boost to their respective group's land banks, as well as dominating position in the property market.[8]

In September 1982, Margaret Thatcher's Beijing visit brought knee-jerk reaction to the Hong Kong community in general and sparked off an emigrant exodus. But the visit hardly caused a stir in the minds of the property magnates, who were quietly waiting for another land-grapping opportunity to surface.

By the time the Sino-British Joint Declaration was signed in December 1984 (a draft of which was signed in September that year), the developer conglomerates were about to hit another jackpot! While the important document, which guarantees an unchanged economic, social and legal system and lifestyle for Hong Kong people for 50 years after the change of sovereignty, caused mixed reaction amongst Hong Kong citizens, developer conglomerates found an accidental treasure embedded in the densely worded dossier. Paragraph 4 of Annex III of the Joint Declaration limited the amount of land that could be granted in any one year to 50 hectares, although it also provided for the setting up of a Land Commission, whose function was to grant, if justified, extra land quota when the ceiling was surpassed. Nevertheless, this land supply restriction would, as it did, give a strong psychological boost to the property market.

The logic was that as land would always be short and thus should naturally command a high price, this would automatically translate into higher property prices. It would therefore be in the public's interest to buy property sooner rather than later. At least this was exactly what developers wished for and would like the community to believe. Once fed into the engine of propaganda, the message did not take long to be spread all over and instilled in the public's mind. Conception then transformed into action by some and action by some became action by many. This chained reaction was to set the stage for a drama of unrestrained greed on the part of developers and speculators, and blind euphoria stemming from herding instinct on the part of the general public. The drama was to be played out over the next twelve years, highlighted with special effects in the 1992-1997 period.

The Joint Declaration indeed was particularly important to some developers, namely those with huge landholdings in the New Territories, like Sun Hung Kai Properties and Henderson Land, as it provided for, amongst other things, an automatic right of extension until June 30, 2047 of New Territories land leases, which were all held on a fixed lease (without renewal right) that expired on June 27, 1997, without payment of an additional premium. This provision was subsequently enacted into law in January 1988 (the New Territories Leases (Extension) Ordinance (Cap.150)).

In general, it was apparent that the Joint Declaration had a lifting effect on the property market, which had undergone a two-year slump immediately prior to the signing of the Declaration, triggered by the infamous Carrian scandal and the closure of a few banks. Making matters worse was the astronomical level of interest rates, which stood at around 20 per cent at that time. Also, political uncertainties about the coming sovereignty change were just as unsettling. It was not surprising that the Lands Department had to try to sell land by way of a "reserve list" (now called the "application list") instead of through the normal public auction method during that slump period. The "reserve list" method was one whereby a potential bidder or bidders could contact the Department to reserve a site they had an interest in by payment of an agreed deposit. It was only upon receipt of at least one such deposit, which meant there was at least one bidder, that the Department would make arrangements for an auction to be held. By the New Year 1985, almost immediately after Margaret Thatcher and Deng Xiaoping inked the Joint Declaration, the Department received numerous requests for sites on the "reserve list" to be put up for sale, including the prime Admiralty site on which now stands Pacific Place.

Apart from Swire Pacific swooping down to snatch that prime urban site, other developers were just as agile in taking action, as if they knew fully well what the 50-hectare a year land supply quota would do to the property market.

Towards the end of 1984, Cheung Kong Holdings concluded premium negotiations with government on the sprawling Whampoa Gardens site (an old dockyard) in Hung Hom. The project was one of the largest private housing estates in urban Kowloon, with 11,224 residential units in 94 towers and a 1.69 million square feet shopping center. It was completed in phases between 1985 and 1989.[9]

In December 1984, New World Development reached agreement with the Trade Development Council to develop the Hong Kong Convention and Exhibition Center on the 335,000 square feet Wanchai waterfront site. The whole development consisted of two luxury hotels, one office block and one luxury serviced apartment block, apart from the international standard convention and exhibition facilities, with a total gross floor area of 4.4 million square feet. The project was completed in 1988.

As for Sun Hung Kai Properties and Henderson Land, they had their eyes set in the New Territories, where land was still very cheap and competition for land was relatively lower than in urban areas. Both developers were aggressive buyers of new town development sites as well as land exchange entitlements and agricultural lands in the 1970s and 1980s. Their strategy of hoarding low-cost land paid off in a great way for them as the property market went into stratosphere in the 1992-1997 period.

By now, developer conglomerates already had a very good grasp of how to ride the crests and troughs of every property market cycle. From 1945 to 1984, the Hong Kong property market had experienced five cycles. Typically, a full cycle lasted on average for eight years, consisting of five "up" years and three "down" years. Going with the rhythmic movement of the market, those developers adopted a "buy low and sell high" approach and ended up making far more money than people in most other businesses.

So, after the signing of the Joint Declaration, the property market entered the longest bull phase in its history, lasting for a total of 12 years and peaking, ironically, shortly after the change of sovereignty. Bullish sentiments were so deeply entrenched that the fast rising market remained uninterrupted for the entire period with the exception of minor setbacks in the 1989-1991 (June 4 incident and Gulf War) and 1993-1994 (Chris Patten's adoption of anti-speculation measures) periods. Not only did this bull phase turn already-powerful leading developers into unrivalled giants, it also left the SAR government, at its inception in 1997, some US$22.2 billion richer than originally estimated. The Land Fund established under the Joint Declaration collected a whopping US$25.4 billion in land sale revenue with accrued interest during the transition period.

This property bull phase coincided with Hong Kong's booming economy that resulted from a smooth transition from a manufacturing base into an entrepot serving the Pearl River Delta, and then into a full-fledged service economy with export, finance and tourism being its major pillars.

Helped by China's open-door policy in the late 1970s, manufacturers in Hong Kong began moving north across the border into the Pearl River Delta region to take advantage of low labor and land costs there. The money they made from the lucrative export and re-export trade was channeled back into the Hong Kong economy in the form of investments in property and stocks. By the early 1980s, an actively traded stock market in turn attracted the attention of the international financial community and foreign stockbrokers scrambled to set up shop here. After the internationally televised signing of the Joint Declaration, Hong Kong became a major tourist attraction as people from all over the world flocked here to get a glimpse of this vibrant British colony that was about to revert to Chinese rule. In short, money was flowing into Hong Kong from all directions.

Then came the 1990s. By this time, the enviable profits made by developer conglomerates caused, not only smaller players but amateurs too, to want to get a piece of the property cake. Every session of government land auction drew big crowds. Bidding was so aggressive that it took hours to close one session. Many developers with mainland backing and capital were often seen bidding with zest at these auctions. There seemed to be never enough of sites to satisfy the demands of the eager bidders. Who could blame them? Property prices shot up almost 30 per cent immediately after the announcement by government in 1992 of the planned Chek Lap Kok airport construction. They then doubled, tripled and in many cases quadrupled in the run-up to mid-1997. If the first half of the 12-year property bull phase (1985- 1991) was characterized by sturdy upward movements underlined by Hong Kong people's income and savings growth, the latter half could be said to be marked by violent upward thrusts driven by the general public's manic speculation and greed, spurred on by developers' "cheerleader-like" marketing techniques.

At the height of the market, a small apartment (about 600 square feet) in the urban area would cost HK$5 million (US$645,000) or thereabouts, or over HK$8,000 (US$1,030) per square foot. A similar unit in the New Territories would cost about HK$6,000 (US$774) per square foot on average. Urban luxury apartments were priced as high as HK$30,000 (US$3,870) per square foot at the peak while rustic ones traded at over HK$10,000 (US$1,290) per square foot. A luxury apartment with 1,000 square feet floor area in an upscale urban district could easily fetch HK$15 million to HK$20 million (US$1.94 million to US$2.58 million).

Indeed, a few similarities can be drawn from this "propertymania" in the 1992-1997 period and the tulipmania in the Netherlands in the 17th century. When the tulip-bulb market reached its height in late 1636 and early 1637, people mortgaged their homes and industries in order to buy the bulbs for resale at higher prices.[10] Likewise, when the property market was near its peak, people in Hong Kong used their owner-occupier homes (or first homes) and businesses as collateral for bank loans to buy a second, third or fourth apartment with the intention of reselling them at higher prices later. Before the tulip bubble was formed, tulip-bulb investing was a pass-time for the very wealthy. When the middle class realized how much money the upper class made from buying and selling the bulbs, they wanted to join the game. Soon all tiers of Dutch society were swept up in a tulip trading craze that peaked in 1637. In Hong Kong, investing in a second or third property was something that only the rich could afford before the 1980s. During the manic phase, even office clerks, salespersons and others in the low-income group wanted to make quick money from property speculation, not to mention the middle class who had considerable means to play the game. The Dutch tulip bubble ended in widespread bankruptcies and brought on the destruction of many who had once been the country's leading businessmen.[11] In Hong Kong, the damage was nothing short of endemic, affecting almost the entire middle class as well as many from the low-income group.

As the property market entered its manic phase, leading developer conglomerates had become so dominant, both in terms of financial superiority and market power, that their leading status was virtually beyond challenge. One of their winning "aces" was the possession of a very cheap land bank, including land exchange entitlements and agricultural lands, which they had been building up in the 1970s and 1980s.

The July 1996 Consumer Council study about the competitiveness of the private residential property market found a high degree of market concentration in the new private housing market during the period from 1991 to 1994. It revealed that 61 per cent of new housing supply came from just five developers, 55 per cent was supplied by the top four and 46 per cent by the top three.

The study went on to explain that a high degree of market concentration, coupled with "non-contestability" of the market - meaning there is no threat of new entrants, would signify that there is a risk of abuse of market power. In such a scenario, developers would have an increased chance to charge higher prices and engage in anti-competitive behavior.

The study also demonstrated that the Hong Kong property market was not very contestable. It said that while new entrants had emerged from time to time, no new entrant became major players (i.e. capable of producing 5 per cent or more of the annual supply of new private housing) in the market after 1981. The greatest obstacle was the hefty costs and limited availability of land.

As explained in the study, in the 1993-95 period, individual land lots with good residential development potential sold for HK$2 billion to HK$5 billion (US$258 million to US$645 million) each. However, land banks and land exchange entitlements accumulated by leading developer conglomerates prior to the start of the 12-year bull phase were an unbeatable cheap source of land supply. Even if they put in high bids at government land auctions, they would still have an average cost of land that was much lower than new entrants'. As such, the huge difference in average land costs was by far the toughest of barriers for new entrants. Also, new entrants had to depend on scheduled public auctions for their land supply, while leading developer conglomerates were already sitting on vast land banks and land exchange entitlement holdings, which they could use to tender for government sites. The study also says there is little likelihood that the present market structure will be altered in such a way as to improve market contestability in the foreseeable future.[12]

Gravity finally asserted itself on those astronomical property prices by the end of 1997. The trigger was the Asian currency crisis, which claimed Bangkok as its first victim in July 1997. Attacks by global hedge funds on other East Asian currencies then followed suit. In September that year, it was Hong Kong's turn to come under assault and chaos was the order of the day. In the following months, inter-bank rates shot up, the stock market capitulated and property prices slumped. Except for a few brief flaccid rebounds in the years that followed, the property market doggedly headed south. This was despite government's several attempts to arrest the market decline by announcing to call a temporary halt to land auctions and to cut public housing supplies. Several medium-sized developers got caught in the downdraft and have been teetering on the brink of insolvency. This may sound welcome news for the developer conglomerates, as their dominant market position will become even more entrenched. But it might be the death-knell for market freedom in one sector that concerns a vital maintenance element for Hong Kong people.

By the end of 2002 land prices came down a lot since the bubble had burst and this would have enabled potential new players or existing smaller developers to finally buy land at reasonable costs. Were it not for government's unwarranted intervention, market contestability might have a chance of being improved a little. As things transpired, government stepped in at this juncture with its nine-point plan, which included an imposition of a land sale moratorium for one year. Moreover, government's planned scrapping of the subsidized HOS (also part of the nine-point plan) would ensure the private housing market would be rid of healthy competitive pressure from the public housing sector forever.[13]

The middle class was a major casualty in the property crash. People from this social class are mostly highly-paid professionals, company executives, civil servants, teachers and businessmen. Many of them had spare cash in the bank to invest in property with. Willing and capable, they jumped on the bandwagon with alacrity and easily succumbed to the illusion that there was only one way the property market could go and that was, up. Not hesitating for one moment that there might be huge risks involved by virtue of the fact that it was a highly leveraged game (based on payment terms of 30 per cent downpayment and 70 per cent bank loan), they poured out their savings to use as chips for short-term flipping in the hope of making a quick buck. Some even used their own homes and businesses as collateral for bank loans to increase their stakes in the game.

There were reports in the press almost every day about celebrities and businessmen having made millions or tens of millions in a matter of months. The media, awash with advertisements from developers and property owners, was more than happy to fan the flame. People were simply bombarded on a daily basis with coaxing property advertisements, biased market news and trite analysis. The herding instinct in human nature kept people from thinking straight. Property prices were never too high, as they chased happily after upward spiraling land prices, orchestrated at auctions by crowds of new players, small- to medium-sized developers and developer conglomerates. In the height of hysteria the bombshell was dropped. Interest rate hikes brought on by the currency crisis at the end of 1997 triggered the big crash. Prices slumped more than 30 per cent on one stroke.

In 2003, more than five years away from the debacle, the prices of properties in general came down by 65 per cent or more from the 1997 peak. Those who had been most aggressive in the game were the hardest hit, be they speculators or smaller developers. No one in the game, except perhaps the developer conglomerates, was sober enough to be perceptive of what was going on before the crash.

Party hangovers are never pleasant. In this case, they were exacerbated by the surfacing of hidden sicknesses. The middle class had to deal with a deluge of problems since late 1997, including a sliding property market, a stock market crash caused by a high-tech bubble burst, bankruptcies, residential mortgages in negative equity (meaning the sales price fetched would be insufficient to repay the bank loan), high unemployment and an economy that had been far too dependent on the property sector and had no alternative but to undergo structural change. At the end of 2002, the number of court-ordered bankruptcy cases rose to 25,328, which was 176 per cent higher than a year before. Unemployment was lingering above 7 per cent. The number of residential households in negative equity was steadily rising and was estimated at 130,000 in early 2003. At December 31, 2002, the Hang Seng Index was 18 per cent lower than a year ago, at 9,321, which was 49 per cent down from the historical peak of 18,397 reached in March 2000. Although the economy started to recover in the summer of 2004 and the residential property market has recouped some of its losses, the truth remains that Hong Kong desperately needs economic restructuring as she simply cannot afford to be so reliant on land receipts for her fiscal health and the property sector should not be depended on to lead her economic growth. More importantly, the status quo of the land system and property market structure cannot be allowed to continue if social justice and economic efficiency is ever to prevail in Hong Kong.

Did the crash hurt the leading developer conglomerates too? It certainly did. But only to the extent that they had to make a few write-offs here and there that hardly scratched their profit-making ability. Their balance sheets for the ensuing few years would bear this out. For them it was just a matter of returning from the orbit of grossly abnormal profits back to the earthly realm of less abnormal profits.

As Harrison explains in *The Power in the Land*, land monopoly is the key obstacle to the ideals of eradication of poverty and the development of a social system that enhances self-esteem. He believes that land value taxation would remove that obstacle and restore economic efficiency and social justice. At its present stage of economic evolution, Hong Kong society might find the concept of land value taxation good food for thought.

Land once enriched and empowered the medieval lords. The power in land helped the lords to subdue their vassals to lifelong bondage of poverty, while the rulers aided and abetted on the side. Fast-forward to 21st century Hong Kong, do we not detect a looming danger of middle ages feudalism resurrecting, albeit with a nuance? The abnormal property market behavior of the 1992-1997 period rewarded the leading developer conglomerates so abundantly that they can wield their superior financial power at will and devour even more slices in the economic pie and more land as and when they so wish. They are free to invest their "home made" profits, most of which are life-savings of Hong Kong people, somewhere else at any time if they feel Hong Kong is no longer attractive as a place for investments. Their avaricious land hoarding in the last few decades has given them predatory power in the property sector as well as in other economic sectors. As they drain the economy of hard-earned cash by virtue of their dominant market power in key sectors and thus pricing power, the working class majority becomes more enslaved to poverty. While the property bubble burst did much harm to the once robust middle class, it never caused a stir in the upper class. The power in land has enriched the leading conglomerates but impoverished the majority.

THE MAGIC OF AGRICULTURAL LANDS AND "LETTERS A/B"

Readers would be tempted to ask at this point: what does the land system have to do with developer conglomerates making abnormally huge profits? This subsection and the next will attempt to answer that question.

In accounting terms, business profit is sales revenue minus cost of sales. In the property development business, the preponderant portion of "cost of sales" is land cost. Hence it goes without saying, the lower the cost of land, the higher the profit margin. For small- to medium-size developers whose only way of acquiring land is through bidding at government land auctions or tenders, at best they would only be able to make normal profit, as their land is obtained through competitive bidding. However, for developers who possess large agricultural land holdings, and incidentally these are the few developer conglomerates, the story is entirely different.

As the new town program was becoming insufficient to meet land needs in the 1990s, developer conglomerates' incessant accumulation of agricultural lands in the earlier two decades proved to be a winning tactic. As a result, some have built up an impressive agricultural land bank and would never run out of developable land even if the government stopped selling land for years. Sun Hung Kai Properties owns 24 million square feet while Henderson Land has 32.8 million square feet in stock. As these agricultural lands were usually acquired at negligible costs, their carrying costs were correspondingly low. Developers who are capable of carrying agricultural lands as stock are very strong financially anyway and can more than afford to carry them for long periods of time. A developer would need to pay a premium to government only if and when conversion into residential or other use was deemed appropriate or opportune. These agricultural land holdings are like a form of land purchase option with no time limit and with the "strike price" (i.e. the premium) practically pegged to market (as the conversion timing decision rests with the owner). The only risk is that some agricultural lots might fall within an "agricultural use" zone under statutory zoning plans, which would render those lots useless for development purpose. Even under such circumstances, an application can still be made for rezoning.

Assuming an agricultural lot was zoned "residential", the procedure to follow in the event of a desire to develop that lot would be quite simple. The developer owner of the lot would need to apply for a "lease modification" to basically change the agricultural use stipulated in the land lease into residential or other desired use. Once the application is received by the relevant District Lands Office (DLO), it will be circulated to various government departments like Buildings, Civil Engineering, Highways, Town Planning, Transport, Environmental Protection etc. for their comments. When their comments are collected, DLO will prepare a set of draft terms and conditions for submission to the District Land Conference for approval. Upon the Conference's approval, DLO will send out a letter to the applicant stating the basic terms of modification. If the applicant accepts those terms, then a premium will be assessed and an official "offer letter" will be sent to the applicant, which will be valid for acceptance within six months.

An apparent advantage to the developer lies in the premium assessment, compared with an outright land purchase through auction or tender. The premium is arrived at by subtracting the "before" land value (i.e. based on agricultural use) from the "after" land value (i.e. based on the proposed use). As the final assessment is the result of numerous negotiations between the applicant and government, with each party using its own independent professional valuer, the finally agreed amount is often lower than the original assessment by government. Also, there is no competition involved as in the case of auctions or tenders. It is simply a matter of price haggling between two parties. As well, the developer has absolute control as to the timing of submitting an application. Needless to say, a market trough would be an ideal time to apply for lease modification. Additionally, prudent developer conglomerates would always wait until infrastructure or other public facilities are available in the vicinity of their own lots (e.g. the opening of new MTRC lines or stations) before they would apply for zoning and land use change.

In the case where the proposed use of a piece of land does not conform with the permitted uses (or Column 1 uses) under the respective zoning plan, the first step would be to apply to the Town Planning Board for planning permission for the proposed use. The notes attached to each zoning plan provide for two columns of uses for each type of zoning: Column 1 lists those uses that are always permitted and Column 2 lists the uses that may be permitted on application to the Town Planning Board under Section 16 of the Town Planning Ordinance. Assuming the proposed use is one of those under Column 2, a Section 16 (or planning permission) application is necessary. If and when planning permission is obtained, the next step would be to follow the lease modification procedure described above.

Agricultural land holdings of Sun Hung Kai Properties and Henderson Land together reached 56.8 million square feet by 2009, which is roughly equivalent to 1 per cent of all non-built up lands excluding country parks in Hong Kong.[14] Cheung Kong Holdings owns an agricultural land bank too, although the group has not disclosed the size of that stock. Such huge land holdings, coupled with the groups' overwhelming financial and market power, would ensure their dominating position in the property sector would not be challenged easily in the foreseeable future.

Via the lease modification system, developers with agricultural land holdings will always have an upper hand in terms of land cost versus those without such holdings. One reason is that lease modification premiums are arrived at through negotiation between government and the applicants, as opposed to land being granted to the bidder who offers the highest price in the course of public land auctions or tenders. The other reason is the applicant has absolute discretion as to the timing of the lease modification application. Plainly speaking, it means applicants can always wait for the best timing from their perspective to initiate the application process. This land cost edge possessed by the developer conglomerates was a major factor in helping them achieve colossal profits in the period of property price run-up. Even now, it still remains their trump card.

In order to have a better understanding of how "Letters A/B" (or "land exchange entitlements") were instrumental in bringing huge fortune to Hong Kong's leading developer conglomerates, one would need to know more about the historical background of the creation and subsequent workings of this particular segment of Hong Kong's land administration system.

As urban land supply in Hong Kong and Kowloon was becoming more and more scarce and population was growing at an explosive rate in the 1960s, government initiated a new town development program in the New Territories, with Tsuen Wan as its first target. Development of a new town would usually entail construction of infrastructure, public housing, town halls, schools, hospitals and other public projects, which required the resumption of huge tracts of land. Before January 1960, when private land had to be resumed for public purpose, cash was paid to the landowner as compensation. From January 1960 to March 1983, a system was in operation whereby a "Letter B" or land exchange entitlement document would be issued which would offer the owner of the piece of private land to be resumed by government a choice of either a cash payment or a future grant of building land in any new town development area in the New Territories at an unspecified future time. Most of the land that was targeted for resumption for new town development purpose was agricultural in status. The "Letter B" stipulates that for every five square feet of agricultural land resumed, two square feet of building land would be granted; and for every square foot of building land resumed, one square foot would be granted in exchange. In practice, almost all landowners chose the land grant option, thus creating a future land grant liability on the part of government.

There was one other type of land exchange entitlement that was called "Letter A". "Letter A" was issued when a landowner voluntarily surrendered his land with vacant possession for public purpose without going through the statutory resumption process. Other redemption terms were the same as those of "Letter B".

All through the 1970s and 1980s, leading developers were avid collectors of "Letters A/B" through engaging various specialized "Letter A/B" land agents who had a network of connections with "Letter A/B" holders (formerly landowners) in the New Territories. By the mid-1970s, the outstanding "Letters A/B" that were unredeemed rose to about 36 million square feet, according to Roger Nissim, author of *Land Administration and Practice in Hong Kong* (1998). By the late 1970s, the speculative price for "Letters A/B" was at its height and the vast majority of "Letters A/B" were purchased by four major developers, the author said. As a large proportion of new land in the New Territories was being taken up for public use under the new town development program, less and less new land for private use was available for "Letters A/B" redemption purpose. Realizing the impact this ever increasing land liability had on future land supply, government stopped issuing "Letters A/B" by March 1983.

In the early 1980s, a huge backlog of unredeemed "Letters A/B" had already formed, and in order to speed up the redemption process, government initiated a public land tendering method via a "monetized scheme" whereby developers could submit "Letters A/B" instead of cash offers to tender for government sites that were put up for public sale, as well as to pay lease modification premiums. By the time the Sino-British Joint Declaration was signed in 1984, it was agreed by both governments that all outstanding "Letter A/B" commitments would be settled by June 1997. As government had to "absorb" the outstanding "Letters A/B" as quickly as possible, the majority of New Territories land sales had to be put aside for "Letters A/B" tender, allowing relatively less sites to be offered via public auction. This gave the four developers a definite comparative advantage over others as such land tenders were in effect restrictive tenders. Sun Hung Kai Properties and Henderson Land were two of the four privileged developers. The other two were private (not listed) developers and they were Nan Fung Development and Chinachem Group.

Such restrictive tenders differed from the normal land tenders in that they were assessed on a "vintage" basis, i.e. the oldest "Letters A/B" submitted in aggregate would score highest in such tenders. A premium, which represented the difference between the value of the land being granted and that of the land surrendered under the "Letters A/B" as at the date of issue, would be charged to the successful bidder.

Apart from the exclusive right to tender for specified government sites, the four major "Letters A/B" holders also enjoyed extraordinary profit margins from the development of such sites, as revealed in the July 1996 Consumer Council study. The study shows that land costs were normally lower for sites purchased through "Letters A/B" tenders than for sites purchased through public auction. Land costs for "Letters A/B" tendered sites constituted only 10 to 20 per cent of the price of a unit. It also says that estimated profit margins for "Letters A/B" tendered sites ranged from 77 to 364 per cent of total development costs while those for auctioned sites ranged from 6 to 109 per cent, based on results of five case studies at project level involving 13 residential developments.

Though it might not have been the British government's intention at the outset to favor developers via the issue of "Letters A/B", this particular land policy had an accidental windfall effect on certain developer conglomerates. A congregation of such factor and others like timing and luck helped create super rich property empires and at the same time gave rise to a more and more uncompetitive operating environment in the property sector.

According to Nissim, the creation of the "Letter A/B" system was due to the fact that in the 1960s and 1970s government could not afford to offer landowners all cash as compensation for the large tracts of land that needed to be resumed for new town development purposes, and the fact that most villagers in the New Territories would prefer land to cash in any case due to their traditional beliefs and values. It was beyond government's imagination that this land exchange system would later become a cradle for speculation and a money printing machine for certain major developers.

So, in the pre-1997 era, certain developer conglomerates had been privileged, unwittingly, by government land policies. Much unfairness had already been woven into the fabric of market structure in the past decades. Going forward, it looks unlikely the deeply entrenched market power of the leading developer conglomerates will be abated. By sitting on vast amounts of the most unique and valuable of natural resources in Hong Kong and possessing strong financial power, they can afford to wait as long as it takes for the economy to recover from a trough and a whole new bullish market cycle to begin after a bearish one. Most people are forgetful creatures. It would not be long before the pains of the 1997 property bubble burst totally fade out of memory. It would be hard for leading developer conglomerates to become a loser in the game.

LAND EDGE OF UTILITY/BUS COMPANIES

Hong Kong's two electricity companies and gas company, together with Transport International Holdings and First Bus, are all large landowners. The electricity companies own numerous power plant sites while the gas company owns gasworks station sites. The franchised bus companies own a large number of bus depots. They have all either directly or indirectly, at one time or another, engaged in the business of property development (in the case of First Bus, it was its predecessor China Motor Bus who was thus involved), using sites that were or are no longer needed for their original purposes.

That these companies (with the exception of CLP Group) are controlled by large developer conglomerates would make their involvement with the property business a natural course of events. At the time those conglomerates were courting the utility/bus companies, it was probably the latter's land holdings, rather than their core businesses, that they were most covetous about. Of course, their core businesses, being low-risk cash cows by virtue of their monopolistic nature, were no less enticing. Acquisition of those companies gave the conglomerates the best of both worlds: a steady and abundant income stream generated by their low-risk operations plus good growth prospects emanating from their untapped land source.

In all cases, premiums need to be paid for lease modification to convert the original land use to the desired use (mostly residential). Still, these land holdings have provided the controlling entities a relatively cheap land source, giving them a definite competitive edge over those developers who have to rely on government land auctions and tenders for developable land. As premiums for land use change are negotiable as in the case of converting agricultural lands described above, and the landowners can always appeal if they are not satisfied with government's premium offer, development of these lands would often result in profit margins higher than would have been possible had the lands been acquired competitively. Thus, on both counts of land availability and land cost, developers with utility/public bus assets have always had an upper hand.

Examples of well-known private housing estates built on previous power plant sites include City Garden in North Point, South Horizons in Ap Lei Chau and Laguna Verde in Hung Hom. Cases of previous bus depots having been turned into residential projects can be found in Island Place in North Point and Manor Centre in Shamshuipo. Another residential project with over a million square feet floor area in Cheungshawan (next to Mei Foo Sun Chuen) has been built on a Kowloon Motor Bus depot site.

Veteran developers would always be careful about the timing of submitting land use conversion (or lease modification) application to government. Past evidences show that they are skilful in picking market troughs for such submissions. As a lot of these utility-related or bus depot sites are located in urban Hong Kong or Kowloon, developer conglomerates view them as precious assets. And who wouldn't, particularly as developable urban land in Hong Kong is a rarity these days?

Hong Kong people would like to live in a liberal democratic society free of bureaucratic controls. They want to have the ability to create self-employed businesses to challenge the conglomerates that have built their strength on the monopoly control of natural resources. They yearn for an end to poverty and the development of an equitable social system that enhances self-esteem. Yet in the present set of circumstances, where monopolization of land and other key economic sectors by deeply-rooted and powerful conglomerates has become an irreversible trend, those ideals will never stand a chance of turning into reality. People in Hong Kong are dangerously oblivious of the morbid side of economic concentration, which has chiefly arisen from, or at least related to, conglomerates' parasitical monopoly of land, made possible by a socially unjust land system.

As Henry George noted, since no more land can be produced, its exclusive ownership creates a primary condition of monopoly: the existence of barriers to entry. In other words, when a developer buys one piece of land, one piece less will be available for purchase by others. By just sitting on land without doing anything, a developer would stand to gain from land value appreciation arising from the needs of society (e.g. the building of infrastructure). It is this kind of unearned profit that socialists deem parasitical.

People in Hong Kong have long tolerated the unjust exploitation of Hong Kong's most valuable natural resource – land. Developer conglomerates, especially leading ones, have reaped astronomical profits, while government has used huge amounts of public revenue from land sales to feed its oversized civil workforce. Consumers and speculators of property, i.e. ordinary people, are ultimately the biggest losers, as they have discovered in the aftermath of the historic boom and bust. Even under normal circumstances, a buyer is often at a disadvantage as a larger part of market risk is unfairly passed to him/her from the developer, since the latter is allowed to pre-sell flats 20 months before completion of construction. Property buyers in Hong Kong lack basic consumer rights like cooling-off period and building warranties. As such, a buyer is always the weaker party in a transaction that is usually his or her single largest investment of a lifetime.

If Hong Kong people do not want to be reduced to "vassal" status like in feudal times, it is about time for them to do some serious soul-searching. The question to ask is whether they want to be independent persons who know, and are willing to assert, their own rights as consumers. Only by acting in unity as a social group can they expect to achieve any preset goals, the most important of which is urging government to reform the land system, adopt a comprehensive competition policy and laws and to introduce a fairer tax system. Government intervention in the past few years has been conducted in all the wrong places. Where it is most needed, it is lacking. Anti-concentration must become a priority before it is too late.

Chapter 3

Money-Spinners vs. Public Interest

"By far the best proof is experience."

– Sir Francis Bacon

Development-for-sale profit has always been a preponderant portion of overall profit for the mega developer conglomerates, particularly in the better days before the property bubble burst. But it is not the sole income source. One of the revelations of the property bust is that property rental income is a vital stabilizer for these conglomerates in turbulent times. A major portion of their profits comes in the form of rental yields on a large property portfolio held for long term investment. When profit from property trading bears the brunt of sharp market downturns, rental income acts as a snug cushion for their overall profit.

In the decade up to 2002, the three leading developer conglomerates raked in net profits in the total sum of US$40.8 billion. Cheung Kong made an average annual profit of US$2.1 billion during the period;[1] Sun Hung Kai Properties pocketed on average US$1.23 billion per year[2] while Henderson Land made an average annual profit of US$748 million.[3] Apart from the fact that a portion of Cheung Kong's decade-long profits came from Hutchison's extraordinary contributions resulting from the sale of certain telecoms assets, these stratospheric profits all arose from reaping bumper harvests in the property sector. Fundamental components of these profits were development-for-sale profits as well as rental income.

By virtue of the developer conglomerates' dominating market power and pricing strategy, and the lack of consumer rights protection in the property sector, the scale of benefits has always tipped preponderantly in favor of the conglomerates. In a rising market, such imbalance is well hidden as investors and speculators make money as easily as the developers. The moment of truth comes only when the music stops. As time drew nearer to mid-1997, people became blinded with an irrational euphoric sentiment and mesmerized by the sweet pied-piper's tune played by developers and property agents. The happy crowd just followed the deadly tune to their own destruction. What most people lost was not only their lifetime savings, but also their self-esteem.

Apart from enjoying abnormal profits from the sale of pricey flats to the ordinary people, developer conglomerates have also reaped immense benefits from demanding optimal rents from businesses, large and small. Due to their lack of choices and bargaining power, small businesses often find themselves at the mercy of greedy landlords and are driven to desperation as their bottom line gets squeezed by way of having to pay turnover-linked surplus rent. In normal times, their demise would simply lead to quick replacements by some other willing risk-takers.

As most of the leading developers are vertically integrated organizations, property management is one of their major functional departments and at the same time a lucrative area where they assume perpetual control over buyers of their flats. They call this "after-sale service" when in actual fact it is more like extending their profit-making tentacle deeper down the consumer's pocket. In many cases, property management fees of private housing estates are equivalent to 13 to 15 per cent of the monthly rent and they are inelastic too. In better times, property management companies (usually subsidiaries of the developer conglomerates) were able to increase fees annually in accordance with the consumers' price index. However, in a deflationary environment (1998 2003) when flat rents were down by 40 to 50 per cent from their peak, cases of reductions in management fees were seldom heard of. The best that developers were willing to do was to freeze the fees.

Property is hardly the only losing game that consumers play, although it is one that they have the highest stake in. Other areas that affect people's everyday life and where people invariably suffer unfairness as consumers include the use of gas and electricity, public transportation services and consumption of supermarket products. Paradoxically, for the mega conglomerates, these are exactly some of their chief money-spinning tools. By wielding market power in these sectors, often with the blessing of government, the economic lords are able to keep prices of many daily necessities artificially high. Ordinary citizens who live in such a society tragically have no alternative but succumb to subordination to the rich ruling class.

PROPERTY

Housing is critically important to Hong Kong people as a shelter and as an investment. Veteran developer conglomerates know this only too well. Consumer Council's report of 1996 concludes that an entrenched market structure, in which the entry threshold is high, land supply is restricted and dominant developers have great financial power and possess huge land banks, has enabled an oligarchy of developers to adopt supply and pricing techniques to the detriment of consumers. The report quotes government's 1994 Task Force Report as saying that there were prima facie cases of flat supplies hoarding by developers. Because of lack of a monitoring body and competition policy and law, consumers of residential flats have long been taken advantage of. On the contrary, developer conglomerates have benefited abnormally, partly due to a roaring bull market and, to a greater extent, from an uncompetitive market structure.

Apart from gaining colossal profits in supplying shelters to Hong Kong people, developer conglomerates also sit on large rental-producing property portfolios consisting of shopping centers, office properties, hotels, luxury serviced apartments and industrial/office spaces.

For business entrepreneurs, shop rents make up a preponderant portion of business overheads. The amount of shop rent that has to be paid sometimes determines whether a business can stay viable in the long term. For the landlord though, the ability to demand surplus rent when the shop turnover reaches a certain level is far more important than the concern with the shop tenant's survival in the long run. Thus, in boom times when turnover soars, a substantial part of the tenant's profit goes to the landlord as surplus rent, leaving the tenant with less reserves to weather downturns. In bad times, the landlord still gets his base rent even if the tenant registers a loss in his business. Only in very rare cases would a landlord be willing to renegotiate the rent before the tenancy expiry should a tenant make such a request because of business loss over a protracted period. In short, the landlord shares the tenant's profit but never his loss.

Even in bad times, a landlord would rather grant a new tenant (of commercial premises) long rent-free period than adjust the asking rent downward. This is to avoid existing tenants using the adjusted rent as an excuse to request rent reduction on lease renewals and other potential tenants using it as a benchmark reference for new leases. This artificial propping up of the nominal rent is the reason why it normally takes much longer for commercial rents (especially shop rents) than residential rents to come down, after an economic meltdown has set in. Large commercial landlords usually operate in the same manner, exerting influence on market rents. Market forces only take over when supply exceeds demand by a wide stretch, coupled with a protracted period of economic depression. The downward rent adjustment rigidity would not be possible if the market were truly competitive. Yet it is this rigidity that protects large landlords' rental income from short-term market adversity.

Of the economic lords, Sun Hung Kai Properties owns the largest investment property portfolio, consisting of 26.1 million square feet of developed floor area and 18 million square feet of developable floor area at May 31, 2010. The group also owns 25 million square feet of agricultural land, most of which are along the existing or planned railway lines in the New Territories and are or will be undergoing the process of land use conversion. For the half year ended December 31, 2009, the group recorded a net rental income in the amount of US$511 million, compared to a total net profit for that period of US$1.85 billion. The overall occupancy rate was 93 per cent.

Two jewels in the group's investment portfolio are its 47.5 per cent interest (another 47.5 per cent held by Henderson Land Group) in One and Two International Finance Centre located at the MTRC Airport Railway Hong Kong Station and its 100 per cent interest in development packages 3, 5, 6 and 7 at the Kowloon Station of the same railway. The group also owns numerous neighborhood shopping centers in various populous new towns in the New Territories, the more renowned of which are New Town Plaza in Shatin and Metroplaza in Kwai Chung.[4]

The Wharf Group is a lord of commercial landlords in the property sector. It had an investment portfolio consisting of 12.7 million square feet floor area at December 31, 2009. Its crown jewel, Harbour City, situated on the tip of the Tsimshatsui peninsula, consists of 8.4 million square feet of commercial space. The 1.9 million square feet glitzy shopping center boasted of 95 per cent occupancy even in deflationary

2001. Other commercial premises included 4.45 million square feet of Grade-A office, 670,000 square feet of luxury serviced apartments and three hotels. Another commercial gem of the group is Time Square in Causeway Bay, which in recent years has become a hot Chinese tourist attraction. The complex comprises 1.03 million square feet of Grade A office and a 936,000 square feet shopping center. The latter, boosted by tourist shopping, enjoyed a 98 per cent occupancy in 2001. Harbour City and Time Square together make up 51 per cent of the Wharf group's business assets and contributed US$685 million of gross revenue in 2009.[5]

Henderson Land owned a rental property portfolio consisting of 9.4 million square feet of floor area at December 31, 2009, made up of 4.5 million square feet of shopping malls and retail spaces, 3.4 million square feet of office spaces, 900,000 square feet of commercial and industrial spaces, and 600,000 square feet of residential and service apartment spaces. In the 2009 financial year, gross rental income amounted to US$841 million.[6] New World Development had 4.33 million square feet of investment properties (including properties that the group only has partial interest) in the same year.[7] Cheung Kong Holdings had 353,000 square metres of commercial properties for investment/own use in Hong Kong.[8]

By acquiring and owning a piece of well-located land, the landowner is in effect in possession of "spatial monopoly" over that piece of land, due to the existence of barrier to entry and the fact that land is immobile. Banking on their unrivalled financial power, leading developers manage to acquire most ideally located lands, like those adjoining mass transit systems or by the waterfront and thus are able to derive publicly created windfall gains generated by those lands. Land along railway lines would be much more valuable than land that is far away from them. Properties fronting the harbor would have a premium value over those lying inland. Purchaser of these uniquely located lands would capture all the benefits of transport convenience created by public infrastructure and all natural environmental privileges, which would otherwise have been public property. Exclusive ownership of such lands and properties enables the developer-owner to demand extra high rents perpetually from tenants of those lands and properties, simply by virtue of their location. Such unproductive monopoly gains are what social reformers refer to as parasitic income.

Shopping centers that are located in populous districts and enjoy high shoppers traffic have always been developer conglomerates' good milking machines. Tenants of shop units in such shopping centers are often charged a base rent plus any surplus rent that arises when business turnover reaches a certain level. The base rent is the minimum monthly rent that the tenant has to pay and is the negotiated rent. Surplus rent is calculated on a monthly basis as a percentage of that portion of business turnover over and above a mutually agreed level. In other words, if business is good, the landlord gets to share the tenant's gross income. If turnover is below the agreed threshold, the landlord still gets the base rent. Because of fierce competition in many types of retail businesses, entrepreneurs who are desperate to get into a shopping center with good shoppers flow have no alternative but to agree to the landlord's terms. As most well-located district shopping centers are in the hands of the developer conglomerates and other developers who invariably adopt such tenancy practices, retailers have little choice of shop unit locations within a district and little bargaining power.

Good shop location is often the key to success for a retail business. Yet it is the landlord, rather than the retailer, who holds that key. Retailers are thus forced to pay a location premium to landlords in order to get hold of it. To maintain their profit margin, they would, as far as they possibly could, pass on that extra business cost to consumers, who are the ultimate victims of spatial monopoly.

As a business strategy to stay ahead of competition, many retailers have adopted the chain operation model. Under such a model, a number of shop outlets would be set up at the same time, each at a different district shopping center. This is to achieve economies of scale and is one way of spreading the location risk. It is also a means of averaging down the rent. It goes without saying that only the financially strong retailers can afford to employ such a strategy. In order to survive, sometimes this strategy is also used by those who only have marginal financial means. This shows how harsh reality is for the small business entrepreneurs.

Because of unsurpassed holding power, large shopping center landlords can often afford to let shop units stand vacant during temporary market downturns rather than promptly reduce the asking rent. As such, shopping center rentals are not very elastic. As shopping center tenants, many small business entrepreneurs lack bargaining power vis a vis overbearing landlords and are the ones with least staying power when the economy turns bad.

What better business can there be, than just holding golden mile investment properties for rental yield? As reflected in the developer conglomerates' recent balance sheets, rental income was virtually their lifeline in economic downturns. Their monopolistic ownership of prestigious shopping center properties will ensure their domineering power will prevail over retailers and consumers alike.

Another stable, though inconspicuous, source of income for developer conglomerates which also directly affects people's daily lives is property management fee. It is common practice for developers to retain the property management right after a residential project has been sold out. If you think that after paying for your flat, you are done with your financial obligations to the developer, then you cannot be more wrong. On the contrary, you could be indebted to that entity for as long as you are the owner-occupier of your flat, for the property management service that is almost imposed upon you. If you rent out your flat, you can, in good times, make your tenant bear this burden. It is usually written in the Deed of Mutual Covenant, which document is part and parcel of any sale and purchase agreement signed by the buyer, that the developer has the automatic right to manage the common areas of the relevant residential project for an initial period of two years. It is also stated that after that initial period, the flat owners can vote to re-elect the property manager. Experience shows that only in rare cases that the owners' committees would replace the manager, like if the service is found to be sloppy.

In the economic boom times before mid-1997, it was as if by right that property management companies increased management fees annually. It was not uncommon that the annual increments were larger than the annual inflation rates. As people were generally well off and making money was easy, they just were not mindful of such petty outlays like property management fees. In peak times, such fees ran up to as high as HK$2.00 to HK$2.50 (US$0.26 to US$0.32) per square foot of floor area for new projects with a lot of recreational facilities and a relatively small number of units. The average fee stood at about HK$1.50 (US$0.19) per square foot, compared to about HK$0.50 to HK$0.80 (US$0.06 to US$0.10) charged in the 1980s. Since the property market crashed, residential rents came down by about 40 to 50 per cent in the 1998-2002 period. Although many property management companies were forced to freeze their fees in the said period, yet fees in most private housing estates were still at their peak levels despite a deflationary background. It is fair to say though, that the property management business has absorbed a lot of manpower and its existence has at least contributed to an increase in employment of low-skilled labor. Still, consumers are the victims as payers of unjustly high fees, a great portion of which ends up in developers' pocket as fat operating profit. The ultimate explanation is the lack of competition in this business, which again is dominated by the large developer groups.

It hardly needs saying that property management is not confined to the residential sector. Tenants of retail shops and offices developed by the large developer conglomerates are all payers of property management fee. This fee apart, commercial tenants have another big outlay to pay to the landlords, and that is air-conditioning fee. Naturally, profit is also factored into this fee. Some shop tenants have had the experience of having to pay an overall unit fee (management and air-conditioning fee combined per square foot of floor area) that is higher than the unit rent. The range of unit shop rents is very wide, depending on shop size, location, layout and which building level it is on. Rent and overall fee together form a substantial part of total operating costs for the tenant, who has no choice but to pass them on to the consumer.

Imagine you are an ordinary citizen who lives in a self-owned flat within a private housing estate. You scraped all your savings to buy the flat from the developer, in return for which you get the right to occupy the flat. Then every month you have to pay the mortgage and property management fee. Everyday when you go out to eat in a restaurant or fast food shop in the estate's shopping center (which, let us assume, is owned by the same developer), you help the tenant of that shopping center pay his shop rent and fee, which also goes into the pocket of the same developer. On weekends you go shopping in other shopping centers, owned by other developers. Again you help the shop tenants pay their rents and fees by buying consumer items. At the end of the month, can you figure out how much of your monthly salary goes to paying the developers? The answer might be shocking.

ELECTRICITY

Academics like Lam Pun-lee have long contended that Hong Kong people pay too much on electricity bills to the two electricity companies. If consumers pay too much, it can be safely extrapolated that the suppliers earn too much. That this situation has been prevalent is entirely a result of a general lack of competition in the industry and the two companies being protected by what is called "Scheme of Control" arrangements. Since the publication of Lam's book *Competition in Energy* in 1997, CLP Holdings, the larger of the two electric utilities companies, has been offering tariff rebates to customers and has frozen tariff levels. It is not known whether the timing of such action was by coincidence or whether it was taken in response to the conclusions of that publication. Either way, it was at least a gesture of goodwill on the group's part.

The CLP group is the sole electricity supplier in Kowloon and the New Territories, while Hongkong Electric is the sole supplier on Hong Kong Island, Apleichau and Lamma Island. The former had 2.3 million customer accounts in 2009 with a supply area covering 80 per cent of Hong Kong's population.[9] The latter had 563,956 customers in the same year.[10] Publicly listed CLP Holdings is controlled by the Kadoorie family while Hongkong Electric Holdings is a listed company belonging in Li Ka-shing's corporate empire.

In the five years to 2009, CLP Holdings made on average an annual net profit of about US$1.3 billion[11] while Hongkong Electric Holdings turned in an average annual net profit of around US$983 million.[12] Both the companies have, in recent years, diversified into overseas businesses and other non-Scheme of Control areas.

Electricity is a basic necessity for all households as well as for the commercial sector. As Hong Kong transformed from an industrial economy in the late 1970s into a service hub, a rapid surge in electricity demand in the commercial sector was evident. On the other hand, as the economy grew at breakneck speed in the 1980s, a sharp rise in general income level also led to higher domestic electricity demand as the consumption of durable electric goods increased. Currently, the commercial sector accounts for the higher level of consumption of electricity generated.

Lam's study concludes that the equity returns earned by the two electricity companies in Hong Kong are very attractive compared with those in other Asian countries. This can, to a large extent, be explained by the fact that the duopoly operates on favorable terms under the Scheme of Control, according to the professor. He also discovers that the average tariff in Hong Kong compares favorably only with the rates for two out of nine Asian cities / countries (the Philippines and Japan).

Regardless, for the consumer, the relevant question to ask is whether tariff levels could be lower. Based on Lam's findings, the answer to that question is yes, due to Hong Kong's dense population and high level of urbanization.

Put simply, the Scheme of Control is a regulatory contract designed to protect the interests of both the operator and the consumer. Under the Scheme, the electricity companies are permitted to earn a certain minimum rate of return on their fixed assets. But one pitfall of the Scheme is that there is no stated regulatory control over the companies' asset expansion. Government has to rely on its own judgment whether to approve or disapprove their expansion plans. In other words, as long as they can get approval, they can boost their assets and earn a higher return. When they over-invest, consumers have to pay higher prices for unnecessary capacity.

Certain interest groups had long argued that the two companies should not be protected by a guaranteed rate of return. Under pressure from these groups, government made a superficial gesture, when the Scheme came up for renewal in 1998, by requiring the companies to promote demand-side management and energy conservation.

Another pitfall of the Scheme, as Lam points out, is that the electricity companies can manipulate their capital structure to earn an actual rate of return that is above the permitted 15 per cent on their equity capital. This can be done by using debt financing to take advantage of the fixed maximum debt interest rate of 8 per cent on long-term loans and the permitted 13.5 per cent rate of return on debt capital. It also encourages the companies to rely on debt capital rather than equity capital to fund expansion. This loophole is particularly useful when market interest rate levels are higher than 8 per cent. The Scheme is like a licence granted to the two companies to print money, says Lam.

Under the existing structure of the Scheme of Control, where excess returns earned are transferred to the "Development Fund" rather than retained, the two electricity companies have no incentive to lower costs and tariffs, argues Lam. (The "Development Fund" is a reserve which can be used to compensate any shortfall in actual returns.) Also, they tend to, and actually do, operate with high excess capacity, as they have little incentive to promote conservation, given the permitted return is entirely based on fixed assets. The end result is that consumers have to foot unnecessarily large bills.

Under existing arrangements, each of the two electricity companies is a monopoly in its own territory, both in terms of power generation and of power transmission and distribution. Each of them has long established its own extensive transmission and distribution networks. Due to Hong Kong's dense population and highly developed underground traffic, it would virtually be impossible for a new transmission and distribution network to be added. Hence competition is non-existent and will remain so until and unless a new entrant is allowed access to existing networks.

To get around the monopolization of the existing transmission and distribution networks, suggestions have been made for a common carrier system to be introduced. Since the networks of the two companies have been interconnected since 1981 for the purpose of mutual backing-up in case of emergency, it might be possible for the two operators to share each other's networks by paying an access charge. They can thus compete with each other in supplying electricity to all areas of Hong Kong. New entrants should also be allowed to access the networks by payment of a charge.

As for the generation aspect, the two operators could also be made to compete with each other. If one operator can generate electricity at a lower cost than the other, the latter should be obliged to purchase from the former. At the same time, if cheaper electricity is available in areas outside Hong Kong like mainland China, the two operators should be encouraged to purchase from those areas rather than build new power plants in Hong Kong. Such an arrangement would pressure the two operators to lower their costs and tariffs. As well, new entrants should be encouraged to enter the market to compete with the two operators.

Both the electricity companies have, at one time or another, been involved (either directly or indirectly) in the business of property development, as they own numerous sites which house power generating and other auxiliary facilities. Whenever any of these sites are no longer needed for their original purpose, they would be redeveloped, mostly for residential use. So, apart from enjoying monopoly gains from the relatively low-risk utility business, these companies have also been able to grab a bite of the property pie.

In recent years, the two companies have taken active steps to expand their overseas businesses. The Hongkong Electric group has bought various power assets in Australia, while the CLP group has purchased power plants in India, Australia and Thailand. Apparently, demand growth in Hong Kong has reached a plateau and they need to seek out better business opportunities elsewhere. While this may be the most logical decision for any commercial enterprise, Hong Kong people can only lament over their loyal and uninhibited contributions over the decades to the gains of these utilities, who are now happily sowing those gains in some foreign soil.

The only way consumers can hope to benefit as users of electricity is the breaking down of monopolistic power in the sector. Consumers' rights have, to a certain extent, been compromised by government's policies and inadequate monitoring effort, from which the two utility companies have greatly benefited. It is about time for government to review comprehensively its relevant policies and regulations, including the existing Scheme of Control, with a view to remedying any fallacies in the Scheme and introducing much needed competition to the industry.

As electricity is something for which there is no substitute, as far as the user is concerned, fair pricing is all the more important. Consumers have absolutely no choice but to pay what is asked of them. They also do not have a clue as to what the intricacies of the Scheme of Control mean.

Government regulatory power and monitoring effort is all they can rely on to ensure a fair pricing mechanism is in place. But evidence shows that highly paid government officials, either through lack of financial knowledge or common sense, or a general tendency to side with the rich, have failed the general public in carrying out its watchdog duties. As a result, utility groups have been able to reap higher-than-justified profits while consumers have been paying more than a fair charge.

In contrast, electricity deregulation has been a common phenomenon in most developed countries. Both Australia and the U.K. have largely deregulated their electricity sectors and consumers have been the chief beneficiaries. In these countries, deregulation has resulted in an overall decline in prices of about 15 per cent. In some U.S. states such as California and New York, complete retail access to electricity supply has already been available and most other U.S. states are in varying stages of deregulation.[13]

Ontario, the populous Canadian province, enacted the Energy Competition Act in late 1998 to put in place the statutory reforms to dismantle electricity monopoly. The reform process consists of unbundling the transmission and distribution elements from the generation element, subjecting the former to statutory regulations, while splitting up the generation assets and devolving 65 per cent of these to the private sector. In other words, the sale of electricity as a single product is separated from the delivery of it through the transmission and distribution networks. The delivery of electricity will be a regulated process but the sale of it as a commodity will be deregulated. Deregulation was effective from mid-2002. Although the reforms have had their fair share of teething pain, competition theorists are delighted to see the establishment of a long overdue competitive framework.[14]

More recent cases of electricity industry restructuring include Russia and China. At the end of 2002, China announced the establishment of five independent electricity generating and two transmission companies, with an aim to subject the industry to market competition.[15] As an international city operating under "one country, two systems", Hong Kong obviously has no excuse to put off the issue of reforming the electricity sector for much longer.

GAS

The Hong Kong and China Gas Company is the sole supplier of towngas in Hong Kong and is one of the listed companies belonging to the Lee Shau-kee stable. Unlike the two electricity companies, the gas monopoly is not governed by any government regulation. A Consumer Council report issued in 1995 concludes that because of government's laissez-faire policy, the towngas monopolist has been earning excessive profits at the expense of its customers.

Currently the gas company has 1.6 million customer accounts consisting of households and businesses.[16] In the past five years, the company earned on average an annual net profit of US$667 million.[17]

Apart from natural gas used for power generation, two main types of fuel are available in Hong Kong and they are towngas and liquefied petroleum gas (LPG). Natural gas became available in Hong Kong from the end of 1995 but is not used as a domestic fuel. It is used exclusively by CLP for power generation purpose.

According to government statistics, in 1997 towngas accounted for 74 per cent of total fuel gas sold, while LPG made up the remaining 26 per cent. Because of a lack of government intervention, the gas company was able to increase its profit margin from 16 per cent of the average price in the early 1970s to 46 per cent in 1996, based on a study by Lam Pun-lee. He argues that such a high profit margin would not have been possible had there been competition in the gas market.

As people's income rises in tandem with a growing economy, there is a tendency to upgrade the use of household fuels. When they can afford it, they prefer to shift to fuels that are cleaner, more hygienic, more convenient and easier to use. Towngas is of higher quality in comparison to liquid fuels and has become a natural choice for domestic use in cooking and heating. It is also suitable for commercial use in restaurants and hotels. In 1995, domestic consumption made up more than half of total towngas consumption. As more and more new housing developments install gas transmission pipes, there is still much room for growth in market share.

Lam attributes the gas company's ability to gain excessive profits to favorable policies/actions adopted by government. Some of these are the safety laws that facilitated the company rapid development, the granting of land in Tai Po Industrial Estate at very low cost for the building of gas production plants, and the Housing Authority's preferred choice of towngas over LPG for use in public housing estates. Thus, government's attitude and approach was a catalyst in boosting the market power of the gas company. Also, Lam finds that cross elasticity between towngas and other fuels are low and hence the gas company is not subject to "interfuel competition".[18]

The 1995 Consumer Council report also finds that there has been imperfect competition between suppliers of electricity and the gas company due to safety reasons and technical and cultural factors. For example, an alternative to the gas water heater would be the instantaneous type of electric water heater. However, for technical reasons, such water heaters can only be installed in households with a three-phase electrical wiring, which is not common in small- to medium-sized flats in Hong Kong. As a result, most electric water heaters installed in residential flats are an inferior type (water-storage type), which is no match for gas water heaters. Also, the Chinese style of cooking (over open flame) makes gas stoves a preferred choice over electric stoves.[19]

Another obstacle to fair "interfuel competition" is the fact that the gas company is controlled by the Henderson Land group and it is only natural for the latter to promote the use of gas water heaters in their development projects, even if electric water heaters are more cost effective. The same can be said of Hongkong Electric and the Cheung Kong group. Both utility companies may be able to increase their market shares in their respective type of fuel supply by obstructing fair competition.

Against such a background of almost nil competition and a supportive government, another perfect case of an enterprise thriving on monopoly to the detriment of consumers is evident. Lam's study finds that real prices charged by the gas company did not decrease as much as its operating expenses over time. In other words, the company has not shared with its customers the benefits of economy of scale and productivity growth. He also concludes from his study that the gas company (as well as each of the two electricity companies) earned returns in excess of its equity costs in the period from 1979 to 1992. Therefore, there must be some truth in the Consumer Council's allegation that the gas company has been earning excessive profits at the expense of customers.

Since monopoly had enabled the gas company to charge prices and earn returns that are higher than the levels justified by costs, the 1995 Consumer Council report recommended to government to introduce competition to the gas market. The five major recommendations were: (1) To create a common carrier system whereby the gas company would be obliged to allow competitors to have access to its distribution network; (2) Industry players should be encouraged to bring natural gas to Hong Kong; (3) An interim measure of a price-cap regulation as a means of control over the gas company should be introduced before the common carrier system is in place; (4) Property developers should be forced to provide three-phase electrical wiring plus gas piping in new residential developments to allow consumers a real choice; (5) An Energy Commission should be set up to co-ordinate all energy issues and should be advised by an Energy Advisory Committee.

In response to the report, government admitted that the gas company's market share for water heating and cooking fuel was about 50 per cent and still growing. Despite that, it decided not to impose any price or return controls on the monopolist. It merely agreed that the company's tariff setting mechanism should be made more transparent. It did commission an independent consultant to conduct a feasibility study on the creation of a common carrier system.

The consultant report submitted in 1997 recommended to bring natural gas to Hong Kong for competition purpose and to enforce separate accounting treatment of the gas company's transmission and distribution activities and production activities. It also recommended third-party access to the gas company's distribution network (this network can be used to transmit natural gas without any modification).

In June 1998 government issued a statement supporting the establishment of a common carrier system. It also requested the gas company to show its transportation costs separately from other production costs. As for the introduction of natural gas as an alternative fuel supply to Hong Kong, it was content to leave it to private sector initiatives. Without assuming an active leading role in formulating any long-term plan to promote the use of natural gas, the idea of restructuring the gas industry is as well as dead. It goes some way to showing how reluctant government is to change the status quo. At the end of the day, it is always conglomerates' interests that get the most protection and consumers' interests that are placed on the sacrifice altar.

Government's inertia is particularly annoying when the rest of the world is moving fast or has already moved towards utilities deregulation. The gas market is being or has been deregulated in many jurisdictions. Examples are U.K., New York, California, Georgia, Pennsylvania, Maryland, Ontario and Alberta. This means that a householder or a business can buy gas directly from a supplier at a competitive price, not just from the gas utility. The gas utility continues to have the franchise to distribute gas and charge a regulated fee. In all cases, deregulation is effectively the separation of the sale of gas as a commodity from its distribution. The product is available at a competitive price but the delivery is at a standard regulated charge. This would be similar to a situation where you might buy milk by phone and it is delivered by a courier service. The milk is a commodity and it would be priced differently between suppliers, but the supplier relies on a distribution system provided by a truck company. A portion of what you pay would be for the commodity (milk) and a portion for the distribution (delivery fee). In the case of gas, the distribution would remain regulated, but the supply would be a free market.

Based on a Harvard University study, the U.S initiated deregulation of the gas industry at the wholesale level in the mid-1980s resulted in gas prices declining about 35 per cent for large commercial and industrial customers. Prices for residential consumers changed only slightly. Still, deregulation has at least benefited a substantial section of the consumer group.[20]

Since 1999, all gas and electricity customers in the U.K. have been able to choose the company from which to buy their gas and electricity supply. The competitive market has brought considerable savings for consumers, according to the Office of Gas and Electricity Markets (OFGEM). OFGEM is the regulator of the gas and electricity industries in the U.K. and is empowered under the Gas Act 1986, the Electricity Act 1989 and the Utilities Act 2000. The Office licenses and monitors the gas and electricity companies, taking action where necessary to ensure compliance, promotes competition, and regulates areas where competition is not effective by setting price controls and standards.

If only our government is willing to take a look around the world, there is no shortage of examples of utilities deregulation experiences to learn from. If there is a will, there is a way. Consumers in Hong Kong have been dealt an unfair hand for a long long time, and government has been acting like a protector of business interests. Utilities are daily necessities of domestic households. Regulated competition is not only socially just but an absolute must given the advanced stage of development Hong Kong's economy has now evolved into. Accumulation of wealth through exploitation of consumers and abuse of market power should not be tolerated in this society.

Studies have indicated that the production and supply of gas is not naturally monopolistic and should be separated from the transmission and distribution element. Lam supports the 1997 consultant report's conclusion that the introduction of natural gas provides a chance for competition. New natural gas suppliers could, on payment of an access charge, use the gas company's existing distribution network to transmit natural gas. He is of the view that competition in the production and supply of gas would lower the prices paid by consumers. Meanwhile, the gas company could retain control of the transmission and distribution network but the network would be subject to regulation. He also suggests that as a trial phase, government could open certain market segments to competition first, like new developments that require fuel supply. If this proves to be successful, then it could be extended to other areas. Consumers would love to be offered a choice, and if it is one that comes cheaper, so much the better.

SUPERMARKET

For most people in Hong Kong, buying foodstuffs and other daily provisions at supermarkets may be just a daily or weekly domestic ritual. What they may not realize is that their freedom of product choice and bargaining power may have been compromised by the entrenched market structure in the industry, which is characterized by a high concentration of market share. The market is effectively dominated by two powerful chains - Park'N Shop and Wellcome – which control about 70 per cent of sales, with the balance shared by the other 168 supermarket operators, according to the Consumer Council's report of 1994.

The supermarket industry started to mature around 1985, the report says. Since then, the market saw steady growth of the large chains, with Park'N Shop and Wellcome leading the market. Between 1985 and 1993, the annual growth rate in the number of outlets was 5.4 per cent for Park'N Shop and 7.5 per cent for Wellcome. By 1993, the former had 165 outlets while the latter owned 185. The outlets of these two groups together accounted for 62 per cent of the market total. On the other hand, the number of all other supermarket outlets decreased at an annual rate of 4.3 per cent in the same period. The figures demonstrated that the two leading chains likely expanded at the expense of smaller operators, according to the report.

The 70 per cent market share enjoyed by the two chains relative to their 62 per cent share of outlets shows that they have been able to benefit from economies of scale, which new entrants would find difficult or even impossible to achieve. Also, the two big chains have, through expensive large-scale advertising campaigns over a long duration, built up a strong brand name and customer loyalty. This would also be a potential deterrent for new entrants.[21]

One important reason these leading chains were able to maintain high growth rate in a mature market was their close association with their conglomerate parents, who engage in the business of property development. Park'N Shop is the retail food division of A.S. Watson, which is part of the Hutchison/Cheung Kong conglomerate, while Wellcome, operating under Dairy Farm, is part of the Jardine/Hong Kong Land group. It is not hard to detect that Park'N Shop outlets are always found in properties with supermarket facilities and developed by Hutchison or Cheung Kong. Likewise, many Wellcome outlets are housed in Hong Kong Land's developments. As such, not only did spatial monopoly of prime sites allow these chains a big head start over other operators, it has also created another entry barrier for new entrants to the industry. Besides, rental costs in Hong Kong, which account for almost 10 per cent of supermarket operating expenses, are high compared to other places like the U.S., where rent makes up about 1 per cent of total expenses.

A survey conducted by the Consumer Council in 1994 shows that of the 106 public rental housing estates and HOS estates that are equipped with supermarket outlets, 80 per cent of those outlets belong to the two leading supermarket chains.

The current situation points to a market structure where competition is limited as barriers to entry are extremely high. The dominating market position of the two big chains will likely meet no challenge in the foreseeable future. Whether a genuine duopoly market has been formed in Hong Kong is a subject for academics to debate over. However, if competition is restrained in any way, consumers are likely to be paying prices that are higher than justified. Judging from the high growth rate in their number of outlets since 1993, at 37 and 40 per cent respectively for Park'N Shop (226, including other retail shops with different names in the group) and Wellcome (259), it seems their market power has further strengthened at the expense of competition. It is highly probable that consumers have been on a losing streak.

It might be interesting to note that in the U.K., a situation comparable to that in Hong Kong has arisen. According to briefing notes written by Professor Roger Clarke of Cardiff University in 2001, two largest U.K. supermarket chains – Tesco and Sainsbury – accounted for 32.7 per cent of food retail sales in 1996. Their European counterparts registered much lower proportions: 22 per cent in France, 21.4 per cent in Germany and 16.8 per cent in Spain. Clarke concludes that U.K. has a duopoly market structure where a low degree of competition is prevalent. The Competition Commission report of 2000 suggests that U.K. prices are on average 12 to 16 per cent higher than those in France, Germany and Holland, while one press report argues that food prices are 40 per cent higher in the U.K. than in Europe and the U.S.

Clarke's notes also indicate that the leading supermarket chains earned an average rate of return of 16.2 per cent in 1996, which was higher than the industrial average of 11 per cent in the U.K. Such rate of return is not insignificant given the low risk nature of the business.

In Hong Kong, the two-group market concentration ratio of 70 per cent is more than double the 32.7 per cent in the U.K. By extrapolation, consumers in Hong Kong have probably been paying prices higher than justified. Likewise, the leading chains have likely earned returns higher than would have been possible had concentration not been so high.

As Clarke points out in his notes, small suppliers are often vulnerable to anti-competitive practices of large supermarket chains. Experience in the U.K. shows that the large chains are able to exploit their market position to obtain low prices from suppliers with the threat to de-list their products if their demands are not met. The buying power of the leading chains creates the potential for abuse of such power, notes Clarke. It is also common practice for large chains to impose fees and other charges on suppliers. Such market behavior and practice led to an investigation by the U.K. Competition Commission in 2000, which suggested in its October 2000 report the introduction of a new code of conduct to deal with abuse of buying power against small suppliers.

Indeed, other than consumers, suppliers in Hong Kong may also suffer from the market dominance of the two big chains as the latter exert their tremendous bargaining power. The Consumer Council report points out that suppliers have complained that it is normal practice for the big supermarket chains to impose harsh trading terms such as high listing fees, promotional discount, contributions to the promotion fund, loyalty clauses etc. The report cites an example of a leading chain exercising restraint of trade where a supplier was threatened by the chain with retaliatory action if the supplier took part in a Chinese New Year shopping fair, which was viewed as direction competition to the chain's business in peak season. Suppliers are sometimes unable to introduce new products for display on supermarket shelves. Also, overlapping brands in competing supermarkets are getting fewer and fewer due to loyalty clauses imposed on suppliers. The report finds that consumers' choice is limited in the leading chains as these groups tend to follow each other's product types and as a result, new products get less chance of getting onto the shelves. It also says that fewer overlapping brands make it difficult for consumers to make price comparisons between supermarkets.

Another important finding in the Council's report is the practice of resale price maintenance (RPM) among the four major supermarket chains (i.e. the two leading ones together with China Resources and Kitty and Kettie Group). This means that the chains adopt the prices recommended by the suppliers and if any of the chains sell at prices below the recommended prices, the suppliers would withhold supplies to penalize that chain. Because of the industry's adoption of this practice, price competition amongst the supermarket chains is minimal. On the other hand, when the powerful chains wish to increase prices, they often pressure their suppliers into turning to smaller operators to take the lead in increasing prices. In a nutshell, consumers are the ultimate victims of such a market structure that artificially props up prices.

In jurisdictions where competition (or anti-trust) laws are in place, like the U.S., U.K. and most European Union countries, RPM has long been banned as it is an anti-competitive vertical restraint of trade where suppliers require retailers to sell their products at, or above, a specified price. The very existence of RPM in Hong Kong shows that consumers have an uphill battle to fight in achieving a fair pricing mechanism in an industry that concerns their very subsistence.

Ironically, the RPM practice in Hong Kong slammed the door shut on the one chance of introducing true competition to the supermarket industry, when the second largest global chain Carrefour decided to close its short-lived operation here in 2000. The French group had entered the Hong Kong market in 1996 by setting up an outlet in one of the most populous private housing estates, Heng Fa Chuen. Its unhappy experience was epitomized in an official complaint made to the Consumer Council in May 1997 about the anti-competitive price-fixing practices of suppliers. After a round of enquiries, the Council was satisfied that RPM did exist, as stated in its report of September 1997. It was told by suppliers that RPM was a necessary practice to protect their own margins and those of the small shops who would otherwise be forced out of business. However, for the foreign chain, selling below the recommended resale price was vital to establishing a foothold in the industry in view of the high land cost and the entrenched dominant position of the two big chains. Understandably, from Carrefour's viewpoint, RPM is an outdated and unacceptable restraint of trade which should have been outlawed.

According to the 1997 report, suppliers have their own side of the story to tell. They say that if a supermarket marks a price that is below the recommended retail price, other supermarkets would want to match it without sacrificing their own profit margins. It is usual practice for the latter to ask the supplier for a compensatory payment (difference between the recommended price and the lower price). In such cases, the supplier would rather withhold supplies from the discounting supermarket as a punishment than make compensatory payments to the other supermarkets. Also, in the face of financially powerful chains who may bargain for bulk discounts from suppliers and thus may charge customers less than what suppliers charge small shops, suppliers have no choice but to maintain some kind of control over the retail price to prevent the erosion of their own margin. (If small shops can buy cheaper from the supermarket at the retail price than from the supplier at the wholesale price, they would just stop buying directly from the supplier, thus lowering the latter's average profit margin.) As rational a pricing policy as it may seem for the suppliers in the supermarket industry, RPM nevertheless represents an anti-competitive market practice that impedes the efficient working of the industry, and above all, hurts the interests of consumers.[22]

The Council also wrote that such RPM practice should be examined by a competition authority and that such an authority should be set up in Hong Kong. Unfortunately, the Council's recommendations only fell on deaf ears. Was it because of the inaction on the part of government to address the issue that Carrefour decided to opt out? Yes or no, the French group's choice to leave can only be bad news for Hong Kong consumers. It is also the worst signal Hong Kong can send out to the world that an internationally known group, for whatever reason, should find it impossible to continue operating here.

PUBLIC BUS SERVICES

Hong Kong's two largest public bus franchisees are companies controlled by developer conglomerates. Publicly listed Transport International Holdings is a Sun Hung Kai Properties subsidiary while New World First Bus is controlled by the New World Development group. Franchised bus services account for over one-third of the public transport passenger flow in Hong Kong.

Although competition is said to come from other modes of transport, the established network of public bus routes and the lower fare charged by public buses relative to railways and public light buses make public bus transport the preferred choice for most people in the low- to middle-income working class. As such, one item of the ordinary people's daily necessities – means of transport – is effectively in the controlling hands of the economic lords.

A Profit Control Scheme under the Public Bus Services Ordinance sets out a permitted rate of return based on the operator's average net fixed assets. In 1997, the permitted rate of return was set at 13%. Prior to 1997, the bus operators had enjoyed a 16% rate of return. As the profit was linked to their average net fixed assets, they had an incentive to boost their asset base (acquire more buses) regardless of need. It also meant that they had little incentive to reduce fares.

From December 2000, franchisees have had to observe a "Modified Basket of Factors (MBOF) approach when they apply for fare increase, whereby the Composite Consumer Price Index (CCPI) would be used as a reference to indicate public acceptability.[23] But the Public Bus Services Ordinance does not include any specific fare reduction regulation. Thus, even against a deflationary backdrop in the 1998-2002 period, government could do practically nothing to force public bus operators to reduce fares.

In the 1998-2002 period when the general public wilted under personal financial woes, Kowloon Motor Bus was able to reap an average annual profit of over US$116 million in the five-year period[24] and to achieve a compounded annual profit growth rate of 12.5%. .

It was not until January 2006 that a flexible fare adjustment formula was included in the MBOF, which would at least enable government to initiate a downward fare adjustment in the event that economic conditions warrant it.

The only public-benefiting factor in the MBOF is perhaps the 50% sharing by passengers (presumably in the form of fare concessions) of any surplus return earned by the operators over and above 9.7%, which is the Weighted Average Cost of Capital for the industry.[25] The other factors in the MBOF, according to a Legislative Council Brief dated January 2006, include "changes in operating costs and revenue since the last fare adjustment, forecasts of future costs, revenue and return, the need to provide the operator with a reasonable rate of return, public acceptability and affordability and the quantity and quality of service provided". From the terminology alone, one can't help but perceive that the operators' interests are expressed in much more tangible terms than those of the passengers.

The fare adjustment formula would take into account the Wage Index (which is meant to protect operators from rising staff cost), the CCPI (which reflects prevailing economic conditions) and the operators' productivity gain (which is meant as a moderator to any fare increase). As reasonable as it sounds, the formula is only to be used as a starting reference point for considering fare adjustment but will not be an automatic determinant. The final say in any fare adjustment would still rest solely with the Chief Executive-in-Council, who is elected by an economic elite.

Chapter 4

Land and Competition

"The heart has its reasons which reason knows nothing of."

– Blaise Pascal

The land system in Hong Kong has worked to enrich a privileged few and, coupled with the lack of competition in key sectors, has fueled the process of economic concentration and wealth amassing by that privileged class. Land monopoly has enriched the few and impoverished the majority, thanks to land policies implemented under the colonial government and its laissez-faire approach. In the course, incomparable wealth derived from land monopoly, facilitated by the workings of those policies, has allowed leading developer conglomerates to almost wipe out competition in the property market and amass more wealth through monopolistic endeavors in other economic sectors. At the same time, the absence of a competition law (with appending punitive measures aimed at violators) has encouraged owners of that unequaled landed wealth to act with little inhibition as they tread on the competition territory in the property and other economic sectors. Unregulated, the pendulum of wealth and economic concentration is destined to swing to one extreme end, with predictable dire consequences.

Helped by past supportive government land policies, unwittingly or otherwise, the conglomerates managed to maintain a vicious upward price spiral in the land and property market before the crash - a spiral that starts with high land prices. The process runs like this: higher land prices lead to higher property prices and rents (as the public have been led to believe this is a natural cause-and-effect - developers would never run a money-losing business); higher property prices and rents push up consumer prices generally (as rents are priced into retail goods and services); and higher property and consumer prices give rise to expectations of still higher land prices and so forth.

Besides boosting the prices and rents of developers' final products, and thus their profitability, higher land prices also serve to increase their net asset value, as they already possess huge land banks and large rental property portfolios. The price-chasing carousel was clearly evident in the property boom throughout the 1980s and 1990s and has worked perfectly for the developer conglomerates, as reflected in the stunning profits they made during those years. It also explains why they have been so persistent in lobbying the SAR government to cut land supplies when the market stalls: their all-important goal is to prop up land prices. Once they succeed in nudging up land prices, the upward spiraling cycle would automatically kick off once again, or at least this is what they wish.

In a media interview, Stanley Ho overtly urged government (apparently on behalf of REDA) to restore the high land price policy implemented by the colonial government.[1] High land price resulting from a restrictive land supply system naturally serves to grease the fortune-churning wheel of land-enriched conglomerates. As their landed wealth accumulate, they become increasingly dominant in the property game as well as overbearingly powerful in the economy.

Landed wealth accumulated by the leading conglomerates has, on the one hand, worked against competition within the property sector, because less well capitalized developers would find it impossible to compete for large and well located sites (like the MTRC sites), which would always return handsomely to their owners and which inevitably would all end up in the cash-rich conglomerates' land banks. The result: rich developers get richer. The property game is a capital-intensive one at the outset, made even more exclusive to the big boys over the past decades through their land hoarding techniques and market dominance, and smaller developers are increasingly being squeezed out of the market. Also, the workings of a lease modification system have given them a big edge in terms of relatively low average land costs by virtue of their owning huge agricultural land banks and utility/public service purpose lands.

On the other hand, that landed wealth is also a key obstacle to competition in the overall economy because it has allowed, and will continue to allow, those conglomerates to pick and choose relatively risk-free economic assets that would espouse only financially powerful suitors. These assets are either risk-free monopolies or have land-related components or both. Examples of past acquisitions are enumerated in previous chapters. Experience shows that in most cases the targets of acquisition were either relatively risk-free monopolies or franchises or land-rich empires, which served to build enormous wealth for the acquirers at minimal risks. In each case, the acquisition was brought about merely because few other than the acquirer had the financial prowess to do it. It was definitely financial superiority that enabled the Li family's acquisitions of wealth-spinning assets like Hutchison Whampoa and Hongkong Electric, for example.

In other words, unsurpassed landed wealth has brought, and will continue to bring, more of such assets to the conglomerates. Such kind of unrivalled wealth would allow them to acquire anything that catches their whim. By virtue of such wealth and in the absence of any competition regulations, they can easily stump out competition in almost any economic sector they fancy (if it is not already a monopoly itself), just like what they have done in the property sector. What will be put on the altar block is Hong Kong's economic efficiency, her free market spirit and social justice.

During the property boom, land-rich conglomerates saw wealth pouring in without even the slightest effort. At government land auctions, their representatives would just sit there and watch as land-thirsty smaller developers pushed up land prices through aggressive bidding. At the right moment they would raise their hand once or twice to add a little zest to the bidding, without any genuine intention to purchase. When the auctioneer finally showed his satisfaction with the final bid by three strikes of his gavel, the land-rich powerhouses' net worth would get a nice lift, to the tune of billions of dollars. This, however, did not mean that the powerhouses always abstained from purchasing land at auctions. As a rule, they would only put in aggressive bids when the site on sale was an exclusive piece of gem in terms of size, views and location. And they would always end up getting it, because they could better afford it than others.

It is evident in land transactions that the most valuable sites that are offered for public sale invariably end up being sold to the financially most powerful conglomerates. An example can be found in Sun Hung Kai Properties bagging precious site packages at the best urban Stations along the MTRC Airport Railway. These include Kowloon Station Packages 5, 6 and 7 with a total buildable floor area of 4.68 million square feet in a mixed-use development (consisting of hotels, offices, shopping centers and serviced apartments), Package 3 at the same Station with a residential floor area of 1.07 million square feet, Olympic Station Package 3 with 1.11 million square feet of residential space, and One and Two International Finance Center (47.5 per cent interest) at the Hong Kong Station with an attributable commercial floor area of 2.13 million square feet. All of these developments are located at sites conveniently situated above or near the respective Stations which are key traffic interchanges and have nice harbor views. Monopoly of such golden mile sites means a future income stream is almost guaranteed. The Chinese saying "land is wealth" certainly holds true in a place like land-scarce Hong Kong, but applies no more fittingly than to loaded developer conglomerates. The fact that only three bidders submitted tenders for Kowloon Station Packages 5, 6 and 7 due to the sheer scale of the development goes some way to showing that the property game is in true fact an exclusive game reserved for the few powerhouses.

As things stand, a handful of super powerhouses already have a stranglehold on key economic sectors, which have brought world-class wealth to their patriarchs. It is clear that unequaled wealth, chiefly derived from land, is an enabling weapon for the big boys' asset hunting game. Lack of competition in the sectors that they touched upon has allowed their chosen assets to pile loads of cash upon them. Going forward, whenever opportunity presents itself, it is almost a foregone conclusion that those overlords would use their financial edge again to swallow more economic assets, including land. As long as government embraces a high land price policy through restricting land supplies and shuns the introduction of a competition law, a likely outcome is that this process of insatiable feeding would see the giants grow into monsters, smothering competition and stunting growth in the overall economy until it is sucked dry.

FLAWS IN PAST AND EXISTING LAND AND HOUSING POLICIES

Land is scarce and precious, particularly so in densely populated Hong Kong. As guardian of this valuable resource, government is presumed to have a duty to exercise caution in its disposal and distribution. Hoarding of this public treasure by a few economic lords, coupled with developer-favoring land policies implemented under the colonial administration, has already led to extreme wealth and economic concentration. Meanwhile, Hong Kong has suffered for a long time the dire consequences of a deliberate high land price policy (through government restricting land supplies, in particular the 50-hectare a year limit), which has benefited no one but government and the developer conglomerates. Rents form a preponderant portion of business costs, and high rents resulting from high land prices have hindered local businesses from operating efficiently and have impaired Hong Kong's ability to attract foreign investments.

High residential property prices resulting from high land prices have meant ordinary folks have had to fork out a fortune to own a basic shelter. Also, the biggest irony is, despite residential prices and rents having fallen 65 and 50 per cent respectively in 2002/2003 from their 1997 peak, Hong Kong was named the world's most expensive city in terms of living costs in a survey conducted by Mercer Human Resources Consulting in July 2002. Her living costs were 24.2 per cent higher than New York.

Though office rents came down substantially from their peak, retail rents were much more resistant to downward pressure, as big landlords obstinately refused to give in to retailers' demand for rent reduction, even after the onslaught of the deadly disease SARS which wreaked havoc in the retail sector in Spring 2003. At the end of 2002, retail space in Causeway Bay was ranked the world's third most expensive in terms of rent, according to Laing and Simmons' annual *Main Streets Across the World Study*. For three years in a row up to 2000, Hong Kong was ranked the most expensive retail location in Asia, according to a survey of global retail rents. High business and living costs have taken a toll on Hong Kong's competitiveness in general and would stall economic recovery going forward. At the end of the day government has to ask itself: is the price for propping up the land and property market too high to pay?

Since the scrapping of the controversial "85,000 flats a year" production target, government was seen to be under too much pressure, mainly from lobbying groups in the property industry, to show a clear determination how to go about setting its land and housing policies. Initially, it appeared to have the conviction of a need to bring down property and land prices so as to allow Hong Kong to regain its price competitiveness versus neighboring countries. However, the persistent deflationary spiral and chronic economic woes that gripped Hong Kong since 1998 threw government off balance and put it in a quandary. It was no longer sure which of the two options would be more suitable: to keep land prices low or to drive them higher.

Worse still, its supposedly "remedial" actions indicated nothing short of capitulation under the pressure exerted by large developer conglomerates, as evident in its nine-point plan drawn up in late 2002. It has become almost like a government that is run for them. One plausible reason is of course that it is the sole supplier of new land and is dependent on land revenue as an important source of income, which went as high as over 30 per cent of total revenue in the mid 1990s. The reality of a draining public coffer forced government to resign to the fact that its interests were aligned with those of the large developers, while the majority of Hong Kong people continued to suffer in a distorted social and economic structure.

Though never publicly declared, implicit in government's pro-developer actions seems to be its inclination towards reverting to a high land price policy, or at least a belief that higher land and property prices would be the right cure for Hong Kong's economic malady, having exhausted all other avenues. A rebound in land and property prices would be the easiest way out of the economic doldrums. Not only would it solve the much-dreaded problem of deflation (government seemed to believe that the property price slump was the main cause of deflation), it would also take care of the budget deficit problem and would address the complaints of negative-equity homeowners. If this was in fact government's mentality, then it was dangerously turning a blind eye to the likely effect of igniting another property boom (even a mini-boom), not the least of which would be the developer conglomerates getting an even tighter grip on the property sector and the economy as more hard-earned dollars of the gullible public would again start pouring into their coffers. Another deadly effect would be the eternal loss of Hong Kong's cost competitiveness relative to other Asian cities and some mainland cities.

Being the largest landowner and the sole supplier of public housing in Hong Kong, government has a natural vested interest in the land and property market here. It has always derived a major portion of its revenue from land sales. For this reason, politicians and academics have often alluded to the existence of an alliance between developers, the banks and the government in supporting a high land price policy. Although the superficial reason for suspending land sales, which was one of the key measures in the nine-point plan, was for the public good as it aimed to redress the flat oversupply problem and would halt further price decline, the measure might also be seen in government's own interests.

As one economic strategist has argued, maximizing revenues seems to be the dominant factor in government's land sales decision making process, i.e., when prices are soft, like under depressed market conditions, government would rather not flood the market with land sales. Thus, the one-year suspension of land sales could be considered a self-serving measure, from government's perspective. On top of all, it was one measure that definitely suited the large developers well, who, sitting on vast land holdings and a large inventory of flats, would definitely not want to see depressed land and property prices. It would not be illogical to conclude that government acted under lobbying pressure from this interest group. This public land sale suspension measure, coupled with coordinated cuts in future supply of railway lands, was at the core a revelation of the fact that the interests of government and the large developers are inevitably tied. Needless to say, their interests are preserved at the expense of healthy competition, because smaller developers and would-be new entrants to the property development industry would be denied a chance to boost their land banks at relatively cheap prices.

Developer conglomerates have been able to amass great landed fortunes as a direct result of the operation of the land system. Specific policies like the restrictive Letters A/B tenders, the 50-hectare a year land supply restriction and the system of lease modification for land use change (as applied to agricultural lands and utility or public service purpose lands), have all been instrumental in giving the leading conglomerates a super competitive edge and a market dominating power. Although the first two policies are no longer applicable, the third is still very much a policy that continues to tilt the odds in favor of the powerhouses.

While high land price benefits developers in terms of its boosting effect on property prices and rents, the existing system of lease modification premium assessment also gives developers who possess agricultural lands or utility/public service purpose lands a definite edge in terms of land cost and thus enhances their profit margin. This is a system of land pricing entirely different from public auctions and tenders, which are based on the principle of competitive bidding. Premium assessment for lease modification (or change of use) is done by calculating the differential between the "before" and "after" land values and is subject to negotiations between the Lands Department and the applicant developer. Since there is no "contest" element involved in such land premium, the figure arrived at would invariably be lower than the competitive land price offered at auctions or tenders, all things else being equal. In the negotiating process, each party would use supporting data provided by their own land consultant to argue their case. The final figure that is mutually agreed upon is at best arbitrary, and if the applicant is not satisfied with the negotiated figure, he could always cease the talks at his discretion. Also, the decision as to the timing of submitting an application rests solely with the landowner.

Thus, the developer conglomerates who hold vast agricultural land banks and utility/public service lands have little need to compete for lands with other developers at auctions or tenders, unless the sites offered are very unique in terms of size, location and views. Their land costs on average, whether in a rising or falling market, are unquestionably a lot cheaper than smaller developers and are effectively their winning aces. This important land cost edge that developer conglomerates possess was a product of the workings of the land system and has been an anti-competitive factor embedded deeply in the property market structure. The public is generally unaware of the intricacies of such lease modification system, which has inadvertently worked against competition in the property sector. But government seems to be reluctant to be open about the details of such land transactions. Using technical complexities involved in the premium assessment as an excuse, government has been keeping the public in the dark as to how such premiums are arrived at. Lacking such information, the public has no way of gauging the efficiency or fairness of the lease modification system, which is a crucial part of the entire land system.

Utility and public service companies that own lands that are no longer needed for their original purpose are also beneficiaries under the lease modification system. As much as they have every legal right to diversify into property development business, a key question of social fairness arises here. Why has government not resumed those idled lands (like unused electricity power plant sites, gas station sites and bus depots) and put them to the best social use (including reaping the highest value by auctioning them off), since they were initially granted to the companies solely for their utility or public service operation purpose? As much as these are private treaty land grants, the public should have a right to know the manner in which government disposes of this precious natural resource, which is basically a public asset, including the terms under which the land is granted.

It would not be unreasonable to assume that the land granted for utility or public service purpose should be used strictly for that purpose, and if the land is no longer used for such purpose, it should revert to government to allow for better usage, including auctioning off to reap the highest social and economic value. Under existing land grants, no resumption clause is written in the relevant leases, thus allowing the utility and public service companies to treat those lands as private assets. That means they have the right to apply for conversion of the user of the lands when they are no longer needed for the original purpose. This is another aspect of the land system which works against the overall social interest but which the economic lynchpins take advantage of, making themselves immensely rich in the process.

In letting utility or public service landowners take advantage of their possession of land assets and subsequently turn them into lucrative properties by payment of negotiated premiums, government is in fact prevented from realizing the highest value of this precious natural resource. Should government not review the terms of such land grants? It is appreciated that the existing utility or bus depot land grants are subject to their unexpired land lease term and the owners of those lands can continue to exercise their right to modify the lease. But the terms of future land grants of this type could come under stricter scrutiny. Perhaps a resumption clause might be an appropriate insertion. Although past exploitations of such assets could not be reversed, it is still not too late to right a wrong for the future good in terms of social fairness.

The system of lease modification premium assessment seems to operate behind closed doors with too little transparency for the public interest. These land transactions, though admittedly are privy to government and the applicant, concern the fair value of land and are of obvious interest to the general public, not to mention the fact that the incremental site value (accruing to the benefit of the applicant) is often a direct result of public improvement to the environment arising from social needs. Apart from land receipts from auctions and tenders, modification premium receipts form a large portion of government's land revenue. Government is at least accountable to the public as to the valuation of those modification premiums. Admittedly, more transparency would not change the fact that the system still gives the leading agricultural landowners an edge over other players in terms of land cost. But if government has the conviction of keeping land and property prices low by the release of abundant land supplies and by encouraging competition in the property market, then that edge is likely to become less an effective weapon for the developer conglomerates.

In feudal times, rulers were often the protector of the lords' interests. Together, they tended to exploit the weaker social group – the vassals. Sadly, people in Hong Kong nowadays can perceive a phenomenon reminiscent of those tragic old days, in spite of all the economic successes they have achieved and all the virtues of democracy they have come to learn. The government of Hong Kong is the de facto owner of Hong Kong's most precious resource – land. Not only does it control the supply of new land and the building process, but it also provides public housing for half the population. Therefore, its land and housing policies directly affect the public interest in that everybody needs a shelter. However, it has shown itself a lot more concerned with the interests of powerful developers than with the genuine housing needs of the lower-income class.

One significant measure in the nine-point plan was the indefinite suspension of the subsidized HOS. The reason given for this measure was that government wanted to discontinue its role as a property developer so as not to compete in the mass residential market with private developers. But it was actually sidestepping the truth that the HOS market and the private residential market have always been segregated markets in terms of pricing (HOS flats are priced at a discount to the private market) and there is no question of direct competition between government and private developers. This measure was in effect an anti-social one as low-income first-time buyers who cannot not afford new private flats would now be robbed of a chance to buy less costly new HOS flats from government and would probably be forced to buy older flats in the secondary market. This would suit developers well because increased activity in the lifeless secondary market would at least encourage trade-up buying and help revitalize the then limp primary market.

In essence, this was a short-sighted and blatant pro-developer act by which the welfare of the less privileged class would be sacrificed. Whilst it was appreciated that government should reduce its role as a developer by way of internal retrenchment, yet indefinite suspension of HOS flat sales would mean those eligible and planning to buy such flats would be deprived of that option. It would also mean public housing tenants would be robbed of a chance to move into homeownership in the affordable HOS market should they need to upgrade their living conditions.

As the then University of Wisconsin researcher Yuming Fu pointed out in his research paper of February 2001, the high concentration of new flat supply among a few large developers was a result of several entry barriers to the property development industry in Hong Kong. These were: (1) the high volatility of the property market in Hong Kong – the high price volatility favors large and financially strong developers as they can afford to wait out market downturns to cash in; (2) large developers can enjoy the economies of scale of large-scale projects, made possible by high population density, while small developers or new entrants would be denied such advantages due to their relative financial weakness; (3) restricted supply of land and high land cost make it difficult for new players to enter the market.

Moreover, as property development is a long process and involves significant sunken costs in terms of planning, design and approval, this means that exit cost is high and as such would deter new entrants. Fu concluded that Hong Kong's property development market has a low degree of contestability, and, using an event-study analysis method, he showed that dominant players are able to reap economic (abnormal) profits and exercise market power in the land market due to entry barriers. Such economic profits are the direct cause of increased cost of housing and building space for consumers and firms in Hong Kong. The existence of market power would be a disincentive for the large developers to acquire and develop land at socially efficient level, thereby reducing the elasticity of housing and building supply. He also thought that in the long run, the land market would be more competitive if government could adopt a more liberal land supply policy, which would lower land prices and attract more players to the industry.[2]

But in that market trough situation, government believed it could not tolerate lower land prices as it was already running a ballooning budget deficit. Cutting land supplies would seem the most prudent of options as a way of propping up land and property prices and hence the nine-point plan was adopted. However, such an option was absolutely contradictory to the professed objective of reducing intervention and was seen to benefit no one but the large developer conglomerates, who are also large landowners. Also, being so reliant on land receipts for public revenue would raise the fundamental question of whether such a land disposal policy is sound.

Indeed, former Legislative Councillor Christine Loh voiced objection in 1997 to government's policy of raising revenue through land disposal, which was seen as a relevant reason for keeping land prices high. Her concern was that government unduly used its control over land supply to earn a major portion of its revenue. Also, high land prices were a form of high indirect tax that the average citizen would have to shoulder when he/she bought a property, and this was unfair given government was running a fat budget surplus. When it was running a huge budget deficit, this gave it an even better excuse to manipulate land supplies with a view to pushing up land prices or at least preventing them from declining further. The direct victims of artificially propped up land prices would be home purchasers, smaller industry players and would-be new entrants. In short, undue restriction of land supplies violates the basic principle of competition because an artificial shortage is created to distort market forces.

Loh was also critical of the fact that decisions to allocate new land supply or to restrict supply rested solely with a few government officials and the public was not allowed to participate in any way.[3] In terms of transparency, government at least took a step forward by making long-term land sale programs available to the public in the early 90s. But the decision-making process in this area is still very much a closed-door procedure even now.

In balancing its interests in land revenue and in the common good of society, government could try to see itself more in the role of a guardian of land than in the role of a land owner, at least philosophically. Only when it views itself in this reinvented role can it begin to see the virtues of a low land price policy. Property booms and busts should be avoided at all costs and the only sanguine way to prevent them is to genuinely encourage competition by lowering entry barriers for new players and to keep land prices constant at a relatively low level through the release of abundant land supplies, both for residential and commercial uses. Lower land prices may not necessarily mean less revenue for government, as higher volume may make up the shortfall in prices. Lower land prices would naturally lead to lower property prices and rents, which would in turn encourage buying activities in the residential market as well as business activities in the commercial sector, creating much-needed employment in the process. Lower rents might even induce self-employment, which is at least a way out for the large pool of laid-off middle-aged workers who are unlikely to find employment again.

A deflationary bout was nothing more than a natural adjustment process that would correct the preceding bubble phase in the economic cycle and would allow the previous excesses to be worked off. This much-needed breathing period would be best used to recharge Hong Kong's energy and re-establish her priorities. Like the bubble phase, this deflation phase would also one day pass away. Meanwhile, lower living and business costs would put Hong Kong in a better position to compete nationally with mainland cities as well as internationally with other neighboring countries. Once the economy gears up again, those homeowners in negative equity would not feel as bad as before, because they would be able to see a brighter future and prospects of higher income. The high land price policy held so dearly by the colonial administration should no longer bind the present SAR government. If Hong Kong's economy is ever going to be restructured successfully, it is paramount for government to first reduce its dependence on land receipts for its fiscal revenue and increase the transparency of its land dealings with developers, with the public interest in mind. In other words, it has to eradicate its mindset of being in the same boat as the developer conglomerates.

Tung Chee-hwa, in his Policy Address in January 2003, stressed that the initiatives for economic restructuring should rest with the private sector, while government would focus on developing the hard and soft infrastructure. The following is an excerpt from his speech that defined the role of the government in promoting economic restructuring:-

"The economic restructuring that is sweeping through the world has highlighted the unique role of the government. Whether it is persuading trading partners to open their markets as part of the globalization process, or promoting technological education to facilitate the development of the knowledge-based economy, governments in various countries have assumed a key role of driving the transformation process. As a highly open economy, the use of monetary and fiscal policies in Hong Kong to revitalize economic growth is unlikely to be effective. We have to focus instead on enhancing the competitiveness of our economy. Over the past five years, I have repeatedly stressed that the government has to embark on important initiatives on a macro-level. These include investing heavily in education, upgrading economic infrastructure, promoting innovation and technology, improving the business environment, helping the business sector to develop new markets, actively protecting our ecology and environment and improving our quality of life. Concurrently, we will reinforce our strengths in four main economic pillars – finance, logistics, tourism and producer services sectors. We should also capitalize on the rapid development of our Motherland to hasten our economic restructuring. These are important tasks, necessary not only for economic needs, but also for discharging our responsibilities and making good our pledges to the community."

Though the speech did not touch on the subject of government's land policies, it seemed that Tung carefully omitted to name property as a main economic pillar, which was something worthy of applause. Economic restructuring is a necessary evil that Hong Kong must face up to. Over-reliance on the property sector for economic growth in the past has meant too much time and effort have been wasted already in a sector that does not earn foreign exchange for Hong Kong. That time and effort should have been spent in the training of professionals and skilled labor in other more innovative and knowledge-based sectors. The whole society has been suffering from skills mismatch as it has placed far too much emphasis on the property sector. Finding other suitable economic niche or niches to lessen the economic influence of the property sector seems like almost an insurmountable problem. Hard as it may seem, that ocean still has to be crossed if greener pasture is to be found.

It is crucial for government to accept that high land and property prices are the enemy to any restructuring effort and a hindrance to Hong Kong's competitiveness. A high price scenario would only heighten further the already high level of economic and wealth concentration. If enhancing the competitiveness of Hong Kong's economy is truly government's objective as Tung proclaimed, then its first priority would be to urgently review the present land system and its land and housing policies and their underlying philosophy, which should be centered on social fairness and equality. Indeed, land policy is by far the most important of all government policies as the well-being of all economic sectors as well as the welfare of the whole society hinge upon it.

Echoing Loh's concern about Hong Kong's land policy, the Hong Kong Democratic Foundation's September 1999 newsletter commented that "overall, land is in too short supply for business and residential use, and there are further distortions created by the zoning regime". The Foundation believes, and rightly so, that major reform is needed in the system of land supply and allocation.[4] Both Fu's research paper (2001) and the more dated report (1996) compiled by the Consumer Council came to the same conclusion: that Hong Kong's property development industry has a low degree of contestability and that consumers suffer under existing market structure where leading developers are able to exercise market power. What is most puzzling to the public is that despite all these findings, government still chooses to ignore the fact that serious market distortions do exist in the property industry and that those distortions have already done much damage to the overall interest, in the form of acute market and wealth concentration.

The actions it has taken, exemplary in the nine-point plan, seem to be self-defeating in terms of promoting competition. By cutting land supplies, it has effectively denied small industry players and would-be new entrants a chance to buy land at relatively low costs in a depressed market. Government has actively destroyed a chance for encouraging competition. For small players and new entrants, difficult access to land supplies and high land costs are their biggest challenges and thus, suspension of public land sales, even temporarily, does not help. Government seems content to leave the property market in the controlling hands of an entrenched oligarchy.

In the Consumer Council's 1996 report on the competitiveness of the private residential market, the Council described certain market behavior of major developers as leading to less choice for consumers, higher prices, reduced ability to make price comparisons and, to some extent, allowing developers to influence market atmosphere. One favorite supply technique that was frequently used by developers was the release of flats in batches. For developers, this was to test market reaction, but the effect was regulating supply, which was a form of price discrimination, and it would not be possible in a highly competitive market. The report also pointed out the fact that in the period from January 1994 to May 1996, government issued presale consents for 57 projects involving 40,040 units and only 40 per cent of these were put up for sale, with the remaining 60 per cent either not having been put up for sale or reserved for internal sale. Such deliberate sales-delaying tactics would not be possible in a highly competitive market, noted the Council.

The Council's report also found that the new residential market in Hong Kong was not highly competitive and not very contestable with high entry barriers like restricted land supply and high land cost. It questioned whether the best interests of consumers had been served under the existing market structure. Therefore it recommended that competition should be encouraged to guard against possible abuse of market power by: (1) lowering barriers to entry; (2) introducing measures to prevent anti-competitive market behavior; and (3) facilitating consumers' access to reliable property information.[5] Unfortunately, sound as those recommendations were, they only fell on deaf ears.

In a downbeat economy, the whole society suffers. Obviously the working and low-income class to a much greater extent. Everyone has had his/her own cross to bear. Even in normal times, government's priority should be to try to help the weaker members of society, not the rich and powerful. Such priority would be most crucial in economic hard times. If this fundamental role of a referee is not adhered to, how can government be expected to adopt right and fair policies? Whatever the rationale behind adopting those nine measures was, the summary effect was that government was seen to be protecting the interests of a privileged few at the expense of competitiveness in the property market and to the detriment of society as a whole.

HONG KONG DENIED A COMPETITION LAW

For all the claims that Hong Kong is a world-class city that has a free market economy, her own government has stood in the way of establishing a comprehensive competition policy and relevant law, which would ensure real freedom in the marketplace. The Consumer Council issued a report on competition policy in November 1996 with recommendations, to which government only responded with a "Statement on Competition Policy" and by setting up a so-called "Competition Policy Advisory Group" (COMPAG). The Statement merely said that "government sees no need to enact an all-embracing competition law" and that "COMPAG will invite all government entities to adhere to the Statement" and "government calls upon all businesses to cease existing, and refrain from introducing, restrictive practices that impair economic efficiency or free trade on a voluntary basis". COMPAG was just a non-statutory working group that consisted of nine government officials including the Financial Secretary as Chairman, and one Consumer Council representative. What was farcical was that the decision not to enact competition laws was made based on a survey of opinions, not of the public, but only of professional, trade and business organizations, whose very interests would be at stake should competition laws be introduced. It would appear that consumers' opinions have no place in the minds of government officials.

In a nutshell, despite its superficial support of competition as a means of achieving economic efficiency and free trade and benefiting consumer welfare, government was reluctant to adopt a legislative approach on the competition issue, fearing such would upset the business environment. Its prejudice was illustrated in its rejection of a Fair Competition bill proposed by the Democratic Party in February 2001. The Consumer Council rightly pointed out that competition law was an integral part of policy and legal enforcement was the only transparent and effective way to prevent and deal with restrictive conduct. Yet, despite the Council having laid out hard facts and findings, government remained stubbornly unconvinced that the overall situation warranted any drastic action. It was complacently oblivious of the fact that concentration of economic power in the hands of a few had reached a precarious level and if unchecked, that power would likely be used to stifle competition further. Moreover, most developed economies have competition laws and even newly industrialized economies like South Korea and Taiwan have promulgated such laws.

Like a basic shelter, supermarket purchases, the use of gas and electricity, and public transport are also basic needs in a person's daily life. As described in the previous chapter, land-enriched conglomerates are beneficiary owners of these sectors and reap huge profits risklessly by virtue of outright absence of competition, to the detriment of consumers. The Consumer Council conducted in-depth studies and issued reports in 1994 and 1995 respectively on competition in the supermarket and towngas industries. It also released a research paper in 1997 on RPM in the supermarket industry. Apart from issuing a reply stating its support for the introduction of a common carrier system for natural gas, government did little else that was concrete in dealing with the introduction of competition to the gas industry. Neither has it made any attempt to prohibit restrictive trade practices in the supermarket industry.

Implicit in government's attitude and approach is a clear statement that consumers' welfare only plays second fiddle to conglomerates' interests. Both academics and the Consumer Council have been urging government to examine the Scheme of Control for the two electricity companies with a view to plugging up any loopholes for manipulation. Results of all these findings point to the fact that consumers' welfare has been put on the altar block because of inadequate monitoring of the respective industries by the authorities and a general laissez-faire approach adopted by government.

The Council argued in its 1996 report that a comprehensive competition policy and a body of law could remove barriers to entry and ensure a free operating environment in which operating costs could be kept at a competitive level. It cited the successful introduction of competition to the telecommunications market as clear evidence of how competition could help to bring down prices. For businesses, a comprehensive competition policy could ensure fairness in business conduct, consistency in implementation and reduced regulation. Such a policy would be fair because it would act against anti-competitive practices that could drive industry players out of business. It would be consistent because a single authority would be empowered to implement it under a single set of published rules. It could lead to a reduction of regulation because it could avoid the need to devise new rules and commit new manpower whenever new products or markets were created. Benefits for consumers would include lower prices, product innovations, more choices and improved services. The Council was of the opinion that if Hong Kong did not adopt a comprehensive competition policy, it would be denying itself an effective weapon in the fight to maintain its international competitiveness.

The Council believed that government's sector-specific approach to the promotion of competition was not adequate to allow Hong Kong to cope with the challenges ahead. Such an approach, as it pointed out, would fail to provide comprehensive guidelines for government to promote competitive market structures in a consistent manner, lack uniformity and duplicate government resources, and would cover very few industries. The Council thought that the sector-specific approach was "piece meal" and could not match the changes that were taking place in industries. Some very large and powerful businesses had involvement across different sectors and it might be difficult for various government departments to monitor market conduct and obtain an overall view as to how those businesses influenced competitive activity between different economic sectors. A ready example illustrating that worry can be found in the supermarket industry where land/property ownership of the key players (who straddle the supermarket and property industries) presents a major entry barrier to new competitors.

The Council recommended the enactment of a competition law to cover horizontal and vertical collusive agreements and abuse of dominant position, to be in the form of Articles 1 and 2 as follows: (1) To prohibit explicit agreements between firms that are intended or have the effect of preventing, restricting or distorting competition. These would include horizontal agreements such as those involved in price-fixing cartels, bid-rigging etc. and vertical agreements such as RPM, exclusive dealership, tie-in sales, long-term supply contracts etc.; (2) To prohibit any abuse by one or more undertakings of a dominant position that prevents, restricts or distorts competition. This would address monopoly pricing and vertical restraints such as tie-in sales enforced through market dominance. The Council reckoned that without these articles, the competition legislation would be much less effective and, more importantly, would not be accepted as adequate in the international arena. In addition to these two articles, the Council also recommended the inclusion of an article controlling the abuse of collective dominance and an article for the control of mergers and acquisitions.[6]

In response to the Council's findings and recommendations, government argued that an all-embracing law would not be as flexible as administrative guides or sector-specific codes of conduct, while making empty statements that it was committed to promoting competition in Hong Kong. It cited uncertainties that a general competition law would create, especially amongst the business sector, as one major disadvantage of having a competition law. It also said that it did not believe the extent of horizontal and vertical restraints or abuse of market dominance was so pervasive as to merit general outlawing. In conclusion, it promised to issue a policy statement (and it did) on the objectives of promoting competition and discouraging various forms of restrictive business practices, to request all bureaux and departments to adhere to the statement and to establish COMPAG.[7]

In the 1998 Statement on Competition Policy, government said it "considers competition is best nurtured and sustained by allowing the free play of market forces and keeping intervention to the minimum".[8] When it introduced the nine-point plan in late 2002, it probably forgot what it had said in 1998. Deliberately withholding land supplies, even temporarily, is in itself an anti-competitive and interventionist act that obstructs the free operation of market forces. That action goes some way to showing that government has never been serious about its so-called commitment to competition, especially when the issue at hand affects the interests of the developer conglomerates. So, when it said in the Statement that it would take action only "when market imperfections or distortions limit market accessibility or market contestability, and impair economic efficiency or free trade, to the detriment of the overall interest of Hong Kong", it was only ridiculing itself, because, as evident in the property sector, government itself is a conspirator in allowing those market imperfections and distortions to thrive.

Since its setting up in December 1997, COMPAG never followed up on the issue of market concentration and the existence of RPM practice in the supermarket industry. Neither did it take an active part in fostering the introduction of competition to the towngas industry. The group consisted of nine government members and one Consumer Council member, with zero representation from the private sector. Not that the public expected this non-statutory and non-representative group to accomplish any significant mission, having no clear direction from government, nor any intervening or investigative power. But that it was just a deceiving ploy of government's to create an illusion of an open and receptive attitude towards competition must be loathsome to the general public. Government's true stance on the issue was revealed in its rejection in 2001 of the Democratic Party's proposed Fair Competition bill.

The 1994 Consumer Council report on the supermarket industry concluded that over the years, the market position of the two leading supermarket chains had not been seriously challenged by any new entrants as the present maturity stage of the industry, characterized by slow growing demand, offered little incentives to attract new entrants. It also pointed out that the two chains' association with property developers enabled them to have exclusive access to shop sites within certain large developments, presenting a major barrier for new entrants. Difficulties in accessing prime sites and suppliers, coupled with high start up costs and high rental costs, and economies of scale presently enjoyed by the two leading chains, all worked against would-be new entrants. This is one industry where land/property ownership is one major entry barrier and affects competition in that industry in a direct way.

As a result of findings in the Council's study, it made several recommendations to government, the first of which was to designate a body to monitor the supermarket industry with a view to watching out for any growth in market power which might be detrimental to competition and consumer interests. The Council was concerned, with good reason, about the prospect of a merger between the two leading chains or even a merger between a big and a small supermarket chain, given the market share of the two leading chains together was already a hefty 70 per cent of total sales. Any increase in market concentration, coupled with entry barriers, the lack of alternative distribution channels and existence of restrictive practices, would warrant special attention by government. By way of comparison, the Council pointed out that horizontal mergers in the U.S. would be challenged under their anti-trust laws if they combined over 25 per cent of the market share. The U.K. has similar competition regulations in place. Other recommendations made by the Council included the establishment of a complaint body whose function would be to investigate complaints from both suppliers and retailers regarding restrictive trade practices, and measures to encourage information disclosure for the use and benefit of the industry as a whole.

Any reasonable man would probably find the Council's recommendations rational, constructive and made with consumers' welfare in mind. Yet, without a statutory watchdog body and a uniform set of competition regulations and laws in place, the recommended measures would simply have no chance of being properly implemented.

As for the towngas industry, the Council also issued a report in 1995 and made several recommendations aimed at introducing competition. Major ones included the adoption of a common-carrier system, forcing the gas company to open up its transmission and distribution network to other new gas suppliers, encouraging industry players to bring natural gas to Hong Kong and the establishment of an Energy Commission to co-ordinate all energy issues. After commissioning in 1997 a feasibility study on the introduction of a common-carrier system, government issued a statement in June 1998 in support of a common-carrier system for gas supply in Hong Kong. It stopped short of formulating any active long-term plan to promote the use of natural gas.

As part of an effective competition policy, one of the Consumer Council's recommendations was for government to scrutinize and review statutory monopolies, like the two electricity operators, with an aim to introduce competition at the earliest possible opportunity. Academic Lam Pun-lee pointed out that the Scheme of Control governing the two operators had not been able to restrict their returns on equity capital to a level that is reasonable in relation to the risks involved and the capital invested in and retained in the business. He suggested that some mechanisms to prevent over-expansion of production facilities should be put into place. He believed that in the longer term, a restructuring of the industry would be needed whereby new suppliers should be encouraged to enter the industry while a common carrier system should be introduced to the transmission and distribution side of the business.

Lam argued that before the Scheme expiry date in 2008, an interconnection of the two operators' transmission and distribution networks should be promoted so as to remove the geographical boundaries in the supply of electricity, allowing them to compete with each other. So far, COMPAG's action was limited to conducting a consultancy study in November 1999, which led to further detailed technical study, on increasing interconnection between the two operators. In the 1999/2000 annual report, COMPAG admitted that increased interconnection would require voluntary acceptance by both electricity companies under the current Scheme of Control agreements. This effectively meant there was very little government could do on the issue of competition before 2008.

David Webb commented in his article dated July 13, 2001: "Hong Kong businesses overseas enjoy the fairer opportunities that most developed markets provide through comprehensive competition laws, while at home the government continues to resist calls for such a law. Ultimately it will lose out, as a less efficient market deters foreign businesses from participating in this service-based economy, and the higher costs deter multinationals from locating here. If Hong Kong truly wishes to become a world-class city, then it must adopt world-class competition regulation." He thought that the lack of regulation in the domestic economy permitted a system of entrenched cartels, which effectively impeded economic efficiency.[9]

As regards government's role in the regulation of businesses, the Hong Kong Democratic Foundation reckoned that Hong Kong's internal or non-traded sector was characterized by monopoly and cartel arrangements (HKDF newsletter dated September 1999). Some of these arrangements actually resulted from, or were supported by, government policy, e.g. by the granting of monopoly franchises. The Foundation believed there was unhealthy dominance in the property market by a small number of players. It was of the opinion that a competition law and an authority for enforcement would be needed to protect consumers.

In all the key economic sectors of property, gas, electricity, supermarket sales and public bus services, evidences are overwhelming that competition is either at a dangerously low level or totally absent and consumers have been dealt an unfair hand. Not only are the conglomerates able to exploit consumers due to lack of competition in these sectors, at the same time they heap on loads of cash that could let them stretch their tentacles further into the economy whenever they please. The way government has acted or avoided to act on competition issues involving these sectors seems to be illustrative of its staunch pro-business attitude. Where the interests of business giants and those of the ordinary people clash, it seems that government's choice of position is behind the former.

QUO VADIS?

By straddling the property sector and at least one monopolistic or competition-lacking sector, the economic lords have been able to build tantalizing fortunes that are ranked alongside the world's wealthiest league, thanks to an inherently unfair land system and developer-favoring land and housing policies, the absence of competition regulations and a pro-business government. Put another way, a combination of the workings of the land system and a non-competitive business environment, with government acting as the behind-the-scene director, has created a few economic titans that threaten to grow into ugly monsters. Perhaps it is not so much the powerhouses that ought to be blamed as the system itself. After all, nothing that they have done is illegal. But one thing is certain: if the status quo is to remain, the present social and economic ills will only worsen as the operation of the land system and the lack of competition laws act together to entrench economic and wealth concentration So where do we go from here?

Would Hong Kong people be content to see government forcing up land prices again so that those economic lords' coffers can become even more bloated? It might be argued that homeowners in negative equity would welcome higher land prices, as they might be relieved to see property prices on the rise again. But higher land prices would not be as beneficial to homeowners as they would to the developers. Higher land prices would definitely boost the prices of developers' flat inventories and stimulate activities in the primary market. However, homeowners should bear in mind that Hong Kong's unemployment problem is a structural one and people's buying power and sentiment might not be as strong as they would like to see, which means the secondary market might well stay locked in the doldrums even though the primary market might get some life back. And unemployment will not improve a great deal until economic restructuring is well advanced.

They must face the reality that Hong Kong has to free herself from the claws of property addiction if her economy is ever to stand a chance of going through restructuring successfully. Anyone in the right frame of mind would not like to see Hong Kong fall back into the property trap again, however tempting that might seem. High land and property prices and rents have chipped away Hong Kong's competitiveness and have left her economy to wither, while Hong Kong people are burdened with high consumer prices resulting from high retail/commercial rents. People in Hong Kong must discard the property-biased mentality for the long-term good and honestly work very hard towards finding a way out of the economic straitjacket, whatever that might take. A low cost environment is essential to let Hong Kong regain her competitiveness. Lower land and property prices and rents would be conducive to that environment and it would be in the public interest for government to promote a low land price policy.

Another question Hong Kong people should ask themselves is whether they would prefer to sit back and let the conglomerates continue to take advantage of a business environment that is devoid of competition regulations, while they continue to be exploited in paying more than they should for their basic needs. In economic hard times, wage cuts, massive layoffs, voluntary or involuntary no-pay leave were forced upon Hong Kong people on a daily basis. As though that was not enough pain already, they have had to struggle with unreasonably high prices for supermarket purchases, utilities and bus rides, because they themselves are not protected by any consumer protection law and providers of these goods and services are not regulated by any competition law. While most people suffer as consumers from the lack of such laws, the scales of wealth continue to tip towards the few economic lynchpins as they flourish on the very absence of those laws.

It would not be difficult to imagine the future state of Hong Kong if the status quo is allowed to carry on. Unabated economic concentration is likely to give rise to increased inefficiencies in the economy, ultimately rendering it unproductive and unresponsive. As the economy is drained, the unemployment problem will become prominent and polarization of the rich and poor will reach an unbearable point. An unproductive economy, characterized by high unemployment, coupled with an exceedingly unequal society, cannot but heighten the chances of social unrest and even upheaval, which will be ready to erupt like wildfire with the faintest of a spark.

Chapter 5

Social and Economic Ills

"It is in the knowledge of the genuine conditions of our lives that we must draw our strength to live and our reasons for living."

– Simone de Beauvoir

The land system has unwittingly created an extremely uneven playing field in the property sector, thereby endowing a handful of conglomerates with unrivalled riches. Historical and current workings of the land system, whilst dumping loads of treasure into the pockets of the property cartel, have engendered industrial and economic concentration amongst the same entities. As much as all these three sets of backdrops have nurtured and empowered the same ruling class, each set has created its own clusters of social and economic ills, which may or may not be interlinked but which have become so serious that the need for finding the right cure is now urgent. Assigning all blame to any one party for those ills would be easy but would neither be fair nor constructive.

However, if finger pointing is not going to get Hong Kong anywhere, neither is any procrastination in facing up to the realities of her problems. If it is the systems that have been responsible for most of the malaises, then serious thought should be urgently given to how to go about changing the systems for the benefit of society. If it is the lack of policies and governing laws that have emboldened the elite social group to abuse their position and power to the detriment of the majority, those policies should be implemented and those laws enacted without delay. If inequalities and wealth disparity are so extreme that they threaten the very foundation of a peaceful society, not one minute should be lost in redressing the situation.

Before setting out to find the right solutions to Hong Kong's problems, it might help to take a hard look at the three groups of illnesses that she has been plagued with, which have mushroomed from one or a combination of two or more of the aforementioned settings. Without an objective and accurate diagnosis, any attempt to cure would only beget a more deadly treatment.

CONSEQUENCES OF AN UNJUST LAND SYSTEM

The major flaw in the present land and housing policies lies in government's tendency towards propping up prices by clamping down on land and public housing supplies, though government may not want to admit it. But its action speaks louder. By doing all in its power to halt further land price decline through implementation of the nine-point plan, in particular, through the one-year moratorium slapped on public land auctions and coordinated curbs in railway land supplies, it loudly declared that it did not want to see lower land prices.

Under the plan, even when the moratorium expired, land would only be made available through the "application list" system, which means that only when a developer applies for a site to be auctioned by offering to bid at a certain minimum price, that an auction will subsequently be held for the sale of that site. (The normal practice in the past was to have auctions held in accordance with a pre-set land sale program, while the "application list" system was used as a supplementary option alongside the auction system.) This means that the release of sites, even when made available again from 2004, would be dictated solely by developers' demand.

In effect, government would be handing over to developers the control on the timing of land supplies release, price-setting power and site selection initiatives. This act might inadvertently allow leading developers a chance to manipulate the system. This apart, government's very act of deliberately creating a temporary shortage to prop up land prices ironically goes against its declared objective of minimizing intervention in the market. It also strips small land-thirsty players of a chance to stock up on relatively cheaper sites. The measure is unequivocally both interventionist and anti-competitive in nature and one that is unfairly coordinated by the referee himself in favor of land-rich conglomerates.

By artificially shoring up land prices, not only did government rob the market of an opportunity to adjust naturally and work off the previous excesses thoroughly, it was also seen to have contradicted its pledge of returning cost competitiveness to Hong Kong's economy. A moderated land supply program, one that responds to weaker demand but nonetheless caters to the needs of smaller developers (for example, by means of selling more small lots at auctions), would obviously have been a preferable option to the draconian one-year ban.

Assuming land and property prices do rebound as a result of this land sale ban and operation of the developer-led "application list" system, the chain reaction that results might well push domestic and commercial prices and rents higher and the price chase might start all over again (which seems to have already happened). The consequence is: Hong Kong would perhaps get inflation again, but at the same time would fall right back into the property trap and see her economy forever stripped of the ability to compete in terms of business and living costs. Is this a scenario that government and society would truly wish to see?

While the economy and society continue to be weighed down by the high cost environment induced by the past high land price policy, government still seems to be uncommitted to keeping costs low through adjusting its land policies, both in terms of pricing and land allocation. Artificial price propping through deliberate supply cuts, even temporary, would only be counter-productive (delaying the adjustment process). Keeping land supplies constant when demand is weak with a view to gently guiding prices lower would make more sense.

On allocation, government has never formulated any concrete long-term policy. Pending any decision in this respect, a priority would be to focus on Hong Kong's economic restructuring needs. In other words, where land is needed for a particular economic or industrial innovation or reinvention, land should be made readily available for that purpose and at viable cost, which may mean merely charging a nominal price or a price at a large discount to market, as an incentive to the purchaser. Care should be taken, though, to avoid letting developer conglomerates scoop up cheap lands, using restructuring initiatives just as a bogus excuse.

On the issue of land supply, highly disputable is government's plan to make land available mainly through the "application list" system, which would place too much power in the hands of developers, especially the financially powerful ones, and which is not transparent enough for the public (government does not need to disclose either the applicant's identity or the amount offered for a particular site if the offer is not accepted). There seems to be little reason why the more transparent open auction procedures could not be resumed when the moratorium was lifted.

By ordering indefinite suspension of the HOS, government was in effect handing more market power to the already predominantly powerful developer conglomerates, at the expense of the lower-income class's housing needs. Those who were previously eligible to purchase discounted HOS flats from government would be forced to turn to either the primary or secondary market of private residential flats. While government's retreat from the role of a developer was commended by the private sector as a right step in the direction of non-interventionism, the basic dilemma remains that as a government, it has a duty to provide affordable housing to the less privileged class. Being the largest landowner and sole supplier of new land, property is one sector where government cannot stand totally aloof.

Suspension of the subsidized home scheme, though seemingly done with the aim of reducing intervention in the market, was in reality an adverse interventionist act in the sense that government's withdrawal further distorted an already unbalanced market structure, an act that tilted the odds even more in favor of large developers. In the course, it is the interests of the weaker social class that got hurt. It would make more sense were government's retreat accompanied by a corresponding equalizing measure that would mitigate the void it left. After all, government has always been the single largest developer and supplier of public housing, besides being the sole supplier of new land. As such, government's link with the land and property market is simply not severable and its intervention in the public's interests is only natural. What is important is whether the intervention is done in accordance with the principle of equity and in the interests of a competitive market.

One possible measure replacing the HOS might be the consistent and long-term release of abundant land supplies for affordable housing, which is specifically targeted at the housing needs of the sandwich and lower-income class. If government decides to retreat from the role of a developer of HOS flats, it might consider asking private developers to take up that role. Land for affordable housing could be made available through normal public auctions and special clauses like price discounts or price caps could be written into the Conditions of Sale for this type of land. This would safeguard the availability at all times of affordable housing, take care of the housing needs of the sandwich and lower-income classes and avoid the situation where the developer cartel could assume more market dominating power by banking on the demand shift from the public housing market to the private market.

Affordable housing should be a priority on any responsible government's agenda and Hong Kong is no exception. Apart from demand coming from those who would be eligible under the HOS, another potential source of demand would be public rental housing tenants. About 2 million people now live in public rental housing flats and there is a waiting list of about 130,000.[1] As the economy improves and the need to improve living conditions arises for this low-income class, demand for better quality, but affordable, housing, either owned or rented, would be enormous. Thus, in setting long-term land allocation plans, affordable housing should rank equal in importance with economic restructuring needs. Indefinite suspension of the HOS without any substituting alternatives was neither helpful nor sensible towards fulfilling this important social responsibility. It was a thoughtless act that jeopardized the interests of the less privileged social class..

Needless to say, the immediate goal of such act was to force would-be HOS flat buyers onto the private market, thus helping developers to move their own stock in the limp market at that time. Without HOS flat supplies or other forms of affordable housing, the sandwich and lower-income classes would be denied a chance to improve their living conditions given their limited financial means. If unfortunately they get coerced into buying more expensive private flats due to the unavailability of HOS flats, they would in fact be forced to shoulder a financial burden that is bigger than they could comfortably take on.

A fundamental question of social justice government should ask itself is: why would the rich and powerful warrant more help from government than the weaker social groups? If government refuses to be concerned with the basic housing needs of the lower echelons of society, who else could help those poor souls? It is paramount that government should review its land and housing policies in the light of urgent housing needs of the sandwich and lower-income class, and more importantly, from a social fairness viewpoint.

If current land and housing policies are flawed and likely to cause further chaos in the economy and society, past workings of the land system are just as much to be blamed for the existing social and economic ills.

One apparent anomaly that resulted from the lease modification system, the restrictive Letters A/B land tenders, the 50-hectare a year land supply ceiling and a high land price policy, was the creation of a few super-rich families, who happened to be in the right business at the right time in the right place, and whose wealth now ranks world-class. Overbearing financial and market power possessed by conglomerates under the control of those families has resulted chiefly from accumulation of landed wealth in the past four decades. This financial superiority itself is one big anti-competitive factor prevalent in the property sector and in other sectors that they are involved in.

In the property sector, while their incomparable financial prowess has enabled them to buy, to the exclusion of others, the most valuable sites there are available, they continue to enjoy a comparative land cost edge made possible by the lease modification system – a system that is inherited from the colonial administration, through possession of huge agricultural land banks and utility or public service purpose lands. The conglomerates' wealth supremacy, coupled with a facilitating land system that gives them a land cost edge, has worked to create a lopsided and treacherous playing field, which was a partial cause for the near-demise of a number of medium-sized developer firms in the aftermath of the property crash.

A number of small- to medium-sized players succumbed to defeat since the market crashed in 1998. One main reason contributing to their annihilation is that they did not have a land bank and were forced to bid aggressively for land at government land auctions. As such, they were taking risks much higher than the entrenched group of leading developer conglomerates who possessed large cheap agricultural land banks. Also, their relatively weak financial capabilities compared to the big boys put them in a precarious position when the market made a drastic turn for the worse.

In the 1980s, it was relatively safe to acquire land competitively as the market had just begun a long bull trend. Property prices would always be higher when new projects neared completion than when they started, and thus making a profit was no problem at all. However, when they used the same aggressive land bidding strategy in the 1990s, they were destined to hit a snag when the market turned the corner. As things transpired, the market did slump and left them out in the cold holding expensive sites bought from auctions. Their high debt position forced them to sell at a loss in a down market. In the cases of two medium-sized developers, Paliburg and Lai Sun, a sudden collapse of the property market in 1998 and its inability to recover within a short period of time caused them virtually to lose their shirt.

These incidences go some way to showing that the existing market structure, in which those who already sit on large land banks with a low average cost have a definite edge over those who do not, exhibits an inherently uneven playing field. If even long established groups such as Paliburg and Lai Sun were unable to weather storms, how can any new entrant be expected to compete successfully with the deeply-entrenched cartel? With the near-exit from the property scene of these and other less well-known developers, one thing is certain, and that is, market power will be even more condensed. Holders of such dominant market power are, more likely than not, prone to abuse it. The end result would be a more tightly manoeuvred market under the control of the oligarchy. As the property game becomes more and more exclusive to the dominating few, end users are more than likely to be an exploited consumer group. They are especially vulnerable because of the absence of competition and consumer protection laws in Hong Kong.

It seems apparent that the lease modification system has been instrumental in giving a land cost edge to conglomerates owning huge agricultural land banks and utility or public service lands and that edge has been another key anti-competitive element in the property market. Perhaps the modification premium assessment mechanism needs to be reviewed to ascertain fairness in the valuation method. The first step would, of course, be for government to start disclosing to the public details of final premium calculations.

Through the workings of the lease modification system, developer conglomerates that acquired utility or public service companies have been able to exploit land assets in those companies. Idled utility sites or public bus depots have been converted into lucrative residential or commercial properties via using that system. This brings out the questions of social justice and efficient use of land, the single most valuable natural resource that Hong Kong possesses. Is it fair for utility operators (or their holding companies or parents) to utilize lands for purposes other than those for which the lands were originally granted, i.e. for their utility or public service purposes?

Land is a scarce resource in Hong Kong and should always be put to the best social and economic use, one that reaps the highest value. The modification premium would be a negotiated amount and would not reflect the "contest" value as would be present in a public auction, and thus would not be the highest value paid. Besides, the utility or public service lands were granted for a public purpose, which raises the question as to whether the operator should be entitled to turn those lands into private use in the first place. It would be worthwhile for government to look into this anti-social land practice that has been in place for decades, and which brought tremendous profits to the owning conglomerates. This practice was at least partly responsible for endowing a competitive edge in the utility or public service landowning conglomerates, which has worked against other players unjustly in the property development industry.

Artificial land supply shortage prior to the handover, or a perception of the shortage, triggered by the 50 hectares-a-year land sale ceiling imposed by the Sino-British Joint Declaration, coupled with a high land price policy, was at least partly responsible for fueling the biggest property bubble of a century in the ending decade of Hong Kong's colonial history. It was also a case in point showing the distorting effect that undue restriction of land supplies had on the efficient operation of the market when demand was on the rise. The artificial land curb did the land-rich conglomerates a big favor by letting them play on the public perception of an impending serious shortage in land and housing supplies and take full advantage of the twelve-year property bonanza, during which their profitability was taken to dizzying heights. On the flip side though, the boom and bust caused the middle class in Hong Kong to suffer a collective financial loss so huge that that social class has become almost extinct.

Here is a real life story that best sums up the plight of the middle class since the property market began its precipitous fall more than five years ago. Henry Lee (an alias) had been working for seven years as a senior architect in the projects department of a medium-sized developer firm at the time when the Asian financial crisis struck Hong Kong in late 1997. He just turned 40 that year and was married with two children, aged 10 and 12, who were both studying at an international school. Henry and his wife, Helen (alias), were together making about HK$120,000 (US$15,500) a month and the family led a bourgeois-style life, living in a 1,500 square feet four-bedroom apartment at Mid-levels. The apartment had been bought in the early 1990s and carried a monthly mortgage payment of HK$40,000 (US$5,160). On weekends, the family would be whizzed away in their chic BMW to Beas River Country Club in Sheung Shui, where they would lunch and play tennis or take a dip in the pool. About four nights in a week they would dine out, either at high-class restaurants or at the Jockey Club's plush Happy Valley clubhouse. Helen worked as an investment analyst with a European investment bank and had no time to spare for cooking, much less household chores, which were all entrusted to a Philippine maid. Yearly overseas travel to exotic places was routine for the four-member family. Life was a breeze, until Henry and Helen made one fateful decision in the summer of 1997. Henry had friends in the industry who were making millions of dollars in a matter of months that year by flipping luxury properties, as the property market galloped like a wild horse without reins.

Developers had a way of whetting potential buyers' appetite. They would dribble out flats in small batches and make eager crowds line up in long queues just outside the sales office, creating a heated atmosphere. The next batch would be priced higher, developers would always thus announce, as if to give hints to speculators that making profit by flipping was a certain thing. Another tactic was to bombard the public with promotional advertisements in T.V. and newspapers. Among the developers themselves, there was also an understanding that the launching time of their projects would be staggered, so that competition with each other for buyers would be minimized.

It was the summer holidays and Henry and Helen had spent two weekends visiting luxury residential show flats of projects that were being marketed by leading developers. Getting a Mercedes would be nice, they thought, if they could make a quick speculative profit. Even Philip, Henry's subordinate, was driving a Mercedes as the lucky soul had made a windfall profit from flipping luxury properties. Henry and Helen had their minds set on a luxury project at Shatin, near the racecourse. True, the additional mortgage payment would put a stress on their monthly budget, but as long as they could find another buyer fast, there was not much risk, they thought. Besides, most of their friends seemed to be making quick money from property speculation. If they did not join in the game now, soon their friends would be much better off than themselves. After all, there was only one way the market could go, and that was, up, as land supply was never going to be sufficient to meet housing needs with that 50-hectare limit. At least that was what the developers and property agents were saying.

Everything looked so rosy and it was hard not to believe still better times were to come. Finally, they picked a high-floor unit in the Shatin project with a price tag of HK$8.5 million (US$1.1 million). They poured out all their bank savings, in the sum of HK$2.6 million (US$335,000), to settle the 30 per cent down payment, and took out a mortgage loan on the property in the amount of HK$5.9 million (US$761,000), which entailed a monthly mortgage payment of about HK$50,000 (US$6,450). By the time they completed the deal, it was already August 1997.

Then disaster struck. Before they had time to nurse their shock that stemmed from the stock market crash, triggered by the currency crisis and which made them lose a small fortune, the property market had plunged 50 per cent. They now found themselves in hot water. The market price of their Shatin flat was now only about HK$4.2 million (US$542,000). Even if someone were willing to purchase it at that price, they would still have to come up with HK$1.7 million (US$219,000) to redeem the mortgage before they could sell it. But where would they find that kind of money now, having already emptied their bank account? So, all they could do was to continue with the mortgage payments (totaling HK$90,000 [US$11,600] per month on two mortgage loans) and hope for the best. All unnecessary expenses were cut and they sold their BMW.

To their utter disappointment, the longed-for market recovery never came. Their fortunes took a turn for the worse when Henry got laid off in early 1999 as the company he worked for teetered on the brink of insolvency. They had no alternative but to sell their Mid-levels flat and they moved grudgingly to a small rented flat in Wanchai. Cash from the sale after paying off the bank loan and deducting expenses was woefully little. A few months later, they defaulted on their mortgage payments on their Shatin flat as Helen's salary was cut by 10 per cent due to her company's streamlining measures. By late 2001, Helen was also laid off and the couple was declared bankrupt by their bank.

Far from being an isolated case, the story of Henry and Helen is in fact quite typical of the vicissitudes of the middle class in the 1990s and stretching into the 21st century. Some may be a little bit more fortunate than this couple in that they may still be on a job, but it is life without fun having to shoulder mortgage payments on negative equity loans (in many cases, for two or more flats), with the threat of job loss like a hanging dagger. In retrospect, underlying the investment philosophy of this social class seems to be a misguided addiction to the "property is wealth" belief. A flat was no longer only a shelter, but also one self-enriching vehicle. It is exactly this addiction that developers played upon and used as their profiting opportunity. It is also this addiction that undermined Hong Kong people's entrepreneurial spirit.

No doubt, greed also played an important part in driving people to do illogical things, as evident in all kinds of wealth-related mania, like tulipmania and the South Sea bubble. But perhaps it is the herding instinct that is so hard to overcome. In their frenzy, speculators forgot that property was a highly leveraged game and short-term speculation was no different from high-stake gambling. The tragic thing is, it had taken years for the middle class to accumulate their hard-earned wealth, and yet in many cases it just took one bad decision and an amazingly short time to empty it all. The trauma of descending from "having it all" to "not having at all" is a bitter enough pill to swallow, let alone facing the prospect of a jobless tomorrow.

One key lesson to be learned from the property bubble is that as the sole supplier of the most precious resource – land, not only must government always strive to fulfill social needs for the use of land at all times, it should also be vigilant of any attempt, especially on the part of large developers, to manipulate the public's perception of land and housing supply shortage. With the end of British rule, would it not be appropriate that the high land price policy implemented under that administration also be officially laid to rest for the benefit of society as a whole? Another major lesson from the boom and bust is that a government's laissez-faire approach in the property market, if unsuitably applied, can have catastrophic effects.

The past high land price policy was the culprit in causing a high cost environment, which has stifled entrepreneurial initiatives and deterred foreign investments. How competitive Hong Kong truly is as a place to do business in is best depicted in a *Fortune* magazine article:

"Property is an artificial market made more so by the fact that many of the companies listed on the stock exchange are property firms that pull in even more investment capital. One result: exorbitant rents, which have made Hong Kong one of the most expensive places in the world to do business."[2]

Indeed, despite residential and office rents once came down by a big margin in tandem with property price fell, retail rents in Hong Kong still ranked among the world's highest. Just how exorbitant is Hong Kong's retail rent level? The following comparison with an advanced economy might give some clue. In the third quarter 2002, when the property market was supposedly in its trough, average retail rent in the private market in Hong Kong stood at US$8.84 per square foot per month.[3] Average retail asking rent in the U.S. in the same quarter was US$16.63 per square foot per annum (equivalent to US$1.39 per square foot per month), while that in San Francisco, considered America's most expensive neighborhood and community retail rent market, was US$27.72 per square foot per annum (equal to US$2.31 per square foot per month).[4]

High retail rents lead to high goods and services prices as businessmen have to imbed shop rents in their mark-up, inflating products and services prices unduly. Yet inflated prices would only work against the business as they would discourage buying sentiment and impair the marketability and sales volume of the goods and services. Operation would be particularly difficult in an economic slump such as that prevailing not long ago, where people's purchasing power was at the lowest ebb. Due to the relative inelasticity of Hong Kong shop rents, many retailers were easily elbowed out of the marketplace altogether in economic bad times as business volumes shrinked rapidly in such times.

Yu Pang-chun, chairman of the Hong Kong Retail Management Association, summed up the operation hardship of retailers by saying:

"Given the high cost structure of our industry, in particular areas of retail rentals and labor costs, keeping operational costs low as well as sustaining business growth will continue to be a challenge for all retailers ...... We have seen a lot of worldwide international brands opening up stores in neighboring countries but bypassing Hong Kong. We have also seen prominent international retailers and quality department stores exit Hong Kong's retail market due to high retail rentals and operating costs – for example, Carrefour, Daimaru, Matsuzakaya, Isetan etc."

Local retailers, who were already losing out to shops north of the border in competing for Hong Kong consumers, suffered yet another blow from the SARS outbreak in 2003. However, despite their pleading with conglomerate landlords for a reduction in rent, their request was ignored. In fact, most retail businesses in Hong Kong have been victimized by artificially high rents, which chiefly result from the high land price policy and from dominating landlords exercising market power to keep shop rents at stratospheric levels. Next in line to suffer were employees in the retail sector, who had to bear the brunt of employers' cost reduction measures in a relentlessly deflationary environment. From a survival viewpoint, if you cannot get your landlord to reduce rent, the only alternative left is to axe your staff headcounts and wages.

Office rents, albeit having declined considerably during that period, were still considered high by some international businesses, especially when they could have cheaper alternatives up north. In 2002, Oracle ditched Hong Kong for Shenzhen as the chosen location for setting up their research and development center for their Asia Pacific division. Oracle was likely to set a precedent for other multinationals and they increasingly would take the same step and move their operations and staff into the mainland, where rents are still much more affordable compared to Hong Kong.

Apart from its inflating effect on commercial rents, the high land price policy also made Hong Kong one of the most expensive places to live in. Even after a 65 per cent correction in residential prices, a decent

700 square feet apartment in urban areas in 2002/2003 still would cost somewhere between HK$2 million and HK$3 million (US$258,000 and US$387,000). In the United States, where the GDP per capita was 50 per cent higher and where the housing market was steaming hot, the median resale home price in January 2003 only stood at US$160,400, not to mention the fact that the size of such a home would be about three times larger than an average Hong Kong apartment. Even in the most expensive sunshine State of California, the median price of such a spacious home was just US$336,740.

Despite some quarters saying in 2003 that the affordability ratio in Hong Kong was then at its highest for years, they might have neglected the fact that the historical high unemployment rate and the gloomy economic outlook in 2002 forced general wage levels to slump at a fast pace. Besides, the fact remained that living costs were still very high relative to other comparably livable places in the world. In fact, Hong Kong was named the world's most expensive city in 2002 in terms of living costs by one consulting firm. High living costs mean that Hong Kong people have had to fork out most of their savings plus a very substantial portion of their income just to exchange for a basic need – a decent shelter, leaving them less disposable income for other needs in life.

CONSEQUENCES OF INDUSTRIAL CONCENTRATION

In the conglomerate-controlled sectors of property and supermarket sales, it is obvious that there is a dangerously low level of competition. As for other sectors of gas, electricity and public bus services, which are also conglomerate-owned, these are either natural monopolies or near-monopolies governed by franchises and any hope of introducing competition would depend largely on the initiatives of government. In all cases, due to the absence of competition and consumer protection legislation, Hong Kong people have had to bear with artificially inflated prices, lack of product/service choices, and lack of bargaining power in these sectors. Owing to the absence of a statutory competition authority and a competition law, smaller players in the property and supermarket sales industries have suffered from an uneven playing field, which has at times put them in an untenable situation vis a vis the financially superior dominating players.

Without the monitoring of a competition watchdog body and the operation of a competition law, it is likely that massive job losses could arise as a result of anti-competitive mergers and acquisitions and workers affected would have no protection. If government is unwilling to change its pro-business mentality and its stance on the competition law issue, consumers would have no alternative but continue to bear with injustice in product/service pricing and lack of choices and small and medium enterprises would have less and less survival space. Government only places itself at the risk, though, of being denounced internationally as backward and not moving with the times, if it insists on keeping the status quo.

By monopolizing valuable golden mile commercial properties, leading conglomerates have been able to derive premium or surplus rents from retail shops in those properties in the form of sharing in their tenants' business profits. Spatial monopoly has allowed conglomerates to reap parasitical rents while their tenants have to be satisfied with a lower profit margin to stay in business in good times. In bad times, retailers often face the difficult choice between moving to a cheaper location or cutting staff, as powerful landlords of major shopping centers rarely entertain rent reduction requests from tenants.

It is understandable that businesses have to be cost-efficient in order to survive. Staff retrenchment may sometimes be a necessary evil to keep an enterprise above water. But the harsh fact is that in many cases where shop space is rented, the staff cut option is taken mainly because the retailer is unable to get his landlord to reduce rent and fees. In these cases, workers' job security is sacrificed as a result of inelasticity of shop rents, due to super landlords exercising spatial monopoly power. Moving to a cheaper location would appear to be a viable cost-cutting solution, but moving expenses plus renovation outlays would often be a deterrent to taking such an option.

Also, in a high unemployment and high shop rent background, the laid-off worker who is unable to find another job is denied a chance to at least have a try at self-employment by starting his own business. As monopolized ownership of uniquely located shopping centers is very much a by-product of the past workings of the land system and the entrenched property market structure, the high retail rent situation is probably one that cannot be solved by the operation of a competition law, or in any manner other than the working of overwhelming market forces (e.g. extremely weak demand over a protracted period of time).

In the residential market, market shares are heavily concentrated in the leading conglomerates and competition is barely noticeable. It is highly probable that consumers have been paying more than they should for a shelter. As pointed out by the Consumer Council, consumers in the new residential market have been suffering from less choice, higher prices and reduced ability to make price comparisons due to certain market behavior of major developers, which behavior would not be possible in a highly competitive market. With the annihilation of a few small- to medium-size developers since the property debacle, market share concentration is becoming even more acute, to the further disadvantage of consumers.

In the supermarket industry, not only are consumers made possible victims of market concentration, but new entrants have actually suffered because of it. Apart from Carrefour's incident (described in Chapter Three), the duopoly supermarket chains in Hong Kong have been accused of causing at least one other failed attempt to beat entry barriers of the industry.

"Jimmy Lai's adMart was crushed by the island's two supermarket giants. And such unchecked power could leave the city a Web backwater", says a *Business Week* article. The event in 2000 points not only to a problem for the dotcom business in Hong Kong, but also to the evils of over-concentration of market power in a limited number of major players in the supermarket industry. Lai had a perfect plan: he would shun bricks and mortar by running a virtual store, thus sidestepping the fight for prime retail space – a key entry barrier. He would set up a few tiny outlets scattered around town. Customers would simply phone, fax or clicked in their orders and his fleet of delivery trucks would take the goods to their doors.

By selling groceries at cut-rate prices, Lai was challenging one of Hong Kong's most powerful cartels. adMart was different from Carrefour in that it was run by a local self-made entrepreneur who knows the local rules of game well. Lai had a track record of being a successful business innovator. Giordano International, *Apple Daily Newspaper* and *Next Magazine* were some of his success stories. That adMart failed partly on account of it being an online business would probably not raise any objection, as countless American online grocery stores got wiped out in the dotcom fiasco. But, as Lai complained, his major snag was that his rivals pressured suppliers into avoiding adMart, forcing him to look overseas for products, which increased his business costs.

In the end, the two giants slashed prices to take down adMart. In the words of the *Business Week* article, "adMart tried to challenge longtime players by introducing Hong Kong customers to e-commerce, only to encounter ferocious and, as many adMart fans charged, unfair opposition".[5] Like Carrefour, Lai and adMart had little recourse, since competition law is non-existent in Hong Kong and monopolies are even encouraged by the authorities.

Perhaps Hong Kong consumers have the most to worry about in the long term. The duopoly is virtually making it impossible for newcomers to survive, be they a smaller operation or a large global chain. How competitive can their pricing be, if they are the only players left and with no threat of new entrants? Why is it that government never paid any attention to the complaints filed by Carrefour in 1997 about RPM? Was it out of exasperation at government's inaction that Carrefour decided to withdraw from the SAR in 2000, or was it the high cost environment? Why was government so indifferent to the significance of Carrefour's exit, which points to something far more serious than just another failed business attempt, something that may perhaps signal Hong Kong's inadequacies in providing a suitable operating environment for foreign investors?

That Carrefour is an international group and the world's second largest supermarket chain (after Walmart) makes the case all the more worth investigating into. After all, Hong Kong prides itself in being an international city that welcomes foreign investments. Not only is Carrefour's incident bad news for Hong Kong consumers, it has also hurt the SAR's reputation as a cosmopolitan city that welcomes international players. In a worst-case scenario, it might even cause a waning of global investors' confidence in the local business environment.

Consumers of towngas and electricity have been paying larger bills than they should, while the operators have been pocketing more than their fair returns, thanks to a total absence of competition and a laissez-faire pro-monopolist government. Despite findings by the Consumer Council and academics, government has been acting nonchalantly on the possible introduction of competition to these sectors. It also seems to be reluctant, or to lack the competence, to review existing financial arrangements under which these utilities operate to ensure fairness in the fee structures.

Without a competition law governing anti-competitive mergers and acquisitions, there is no way of preventing predacious conglomerates from gobbling up their rivals in the sectors in which they already own a large stake, thereby further enlarging their market share in those sectors. Such kinds of market-dominating mergers are likely to give rise to job losses as the merged entity tries to achieve synergy. As much as the streamlining measures are meant to bring efficiency to the operation of the merged corporation, all the benefit goes to the powerful acquirer, while the acquisition act itself is harmful to society as a whole as competition would be subdued by it and abuse of market power is likely. Along the way, many workers' jobs (often those in the merger target) and thus their livelihoods are sacrificed.

If you were an employee of PCCW, you would probably understand the trauma brought about by inevitable job cuts resulting from a company merger. Since Richard Li pulled off the shiny deal – acquisition of Cable & Wireless HKT – in August 2000, the number of employees at the merged company sharply decreased from 16,000 at the time of the takeover to about 12,000 in early 2003.[6] Some have attributed the incessant staff cuts in the last two years to the company's need to reduce its mountainous debt and to return to profitability. Others have blamed them on the continuous decline in PCCW's market share in the fixed line business due to deregulation of the telecoms industry, which entailed cost-cutting measures to stay ahead of competitors.

Whatever the reason, the benefit of the job cuts goes to PCCW, period. The victims are the company's sacked employees and their families. Many of those fired were middle-aged professionals and technicians who had spent all their working life at the former telephone company and had little chance of finding another employer. Thousands of jobs were buried, as a phenomenal corporate buyout was staged.

The merger resulted in PCCW achieving dominating market power in the fixed line network business and it led to massive job cuts. It is without question that Richard spent a lot of effort in trying to turn PCCW around after the major setback caused by the dotcom bubble burst in the U.S. and in trying to find a right way forward for the company. In short, he did the right thing for his shareholders. In the course, though, a large number of unlucky employees were discarded, as he tried to repay the huge loans that had been used to buy out this market-leading utility. They can only blame their misfortune on a society that offers no protection whatsoever to the working class. Workers simply have no defense against employers' retrenchment decisions.[7]

The incident of the PCCW-HKT merger is a ringing reminder that the super-powerful families or companies under their control have the ability, both financially and politically, to feed on any economic asset that they fancy, especially those with a market-dominating edge. As long as government does not change its pro-business mentality and its opposing stance to formulating a comprehensive competition policy and legislating that policy, the whole economy will eventually become one big monopoly game. In the meantime, job opportunities will dwindle as anti-competitive mergers continue to take place. As industrial concentration and economic concentration become more pronounced, the survival space for small enterprises will become narrower and narrower until it vanishes altogether.

There is another inequitable side to industrial concentration and that is, a widening income gap amongst salaried employees. Companies operating as monopolies or leading companies in sectors where competition is at a low level are capable of reaping abnormally high profits as a result of the total or partial absence of competition. Consequently, dominant companies in these sectors can afford to pay higher-than-market salaries and bonuses to retain their employees or even to entice employees from rivals. As the dominant companies grow in size and increasingly profitable, through acquiring dominant companies in other sectors in some cases, their employees get increasingly better rewards. The result: employees of the cross-sector conglomerates get increasingly fatter salaries (including bonuses and share options) than their counterparts working at most other companies. Incidentally, the civil workforce also belongs to the fat-salary group as their employer has also been one big earner of abnormal profit by virtue of being the largest land monopolist. This phenomenon is at least a partial reflection of the more and more uneven distribution of income in general.

CONSEQUENCES OF ECONOMIC CONCENTRATION

Hong Kong has always been a place of sharp contrasts. In best manifestation, it is a cross-cultural cosmopolitan city where the east meets the west. In worst, it is a community marked by tantalizing inequality, where the rich few effectively rule over the poor mass. It is this latter contradiction that has stirred up seething social discontent, which has so far mostly been directed at the public administration. Underlying the discontent is the mass's helplessness in the face of government-facilitated economic concentration benefiting an elite group, which has led to a polarization of the rich and poor.

Worsening the already huge disparity of wealth was the 1998 property market crash, which emptied the pockets of many of the middle-income and working class. As there was no factual evidence that their predicament was brought about by the elite class, the poor majority could only point their fingers at government who, in fact, could not evade responsibility for the social and economic mishaps.

However, the social majority's grudge runs deeper than just losing in the property game. Their discontent also stems from being forced, without recourse, to pay unreasonably high prices for their basic daily necessities, like gas, electricity, transportation and supermarket items, particularly in a depressed economic environment. Deep down in their hearts, there is little doubt that most of the money they earn with their hard work somehow has found its way to the pockets of the few powerhouses. The situation became so grave that it was no longer a question of whether or not the social discontent would translate into widespread social unrest. It was only a matter of when.

That discontent deepened so much that many strata of society, including the normally quiet middle class, took to the streets to protest against the pro-conglomerate government and its many callous and unfair policy measures, all taken to protect the powerful and to persecute the weak. The post-colonial era witnessed large-scale public demonstration by teachers, doctors, middle class, social workers, civil servants, welfare recipients, foreign domestic helpers and even old-aged groups.

In the words of Lau Siu-kai, the then Professor of the Hong Kong Institute of Asia Pacific Studies at the Chinese University, "We have an elitist government. Everyone in Hong Kong knows we need reform. But small and middle players feel they must take to the streets because they have no other way to assure their interests are protected."

Perhaps this description of the SAR government by the World Socialist Website said it all, "Tung's administration has proven to be as autocratic, remote and subservient to Hong Kong's powerful business tycoons as the previous British colonial governors." The description seems to be a perfect reflection of what goes on in the hearts and minds of the Hong Kong society at large. For those who were struggling to make ends meet in the high-unemployment environment, it was only natural that they felt a sense of disillusionment, as at the time of the handover the SAR government promised to bring "a future of excellence and prosperity for all".[8]

A CNN.com article painted this vivid social picture of Hong Kong at that time:

"Socially, the SAR is heading towards more conflicts and unrest. With an unemployment rate of 7.4 per cent, the gap between rich and poor is widening. Most Hong Kong Chinese have not taken to the streets because they tend to be politically patient. Their savings can help them live hand to mouth, thus they tolerate misrule to a large extent, even as many organizations in the private and public sectors downsize. However, there is considerable latent discontent, reflected by the relatively poor popularity ratings of top leaders. Another social and economic problem is the intensification of class contradictions. With the poor increasingly casting a jealous eye on many rich business tycoons – who enjoy both economic and political power – the SAR is now encountering the phenomenon of a few frustrated citizens planting bombs and issuing threats to government officials. Social turbulence is likely to persist unless the government takes urgent action to address the income gap. Ironically, with a huge financial deficit, the government is reluctant to antagonize the rich by increasing profits tax. But widening the tax net will mean that more members of the middle and lower classes will be in danger of joining the proletariat. Compounding the problem is the grievance of many middle class citizens, who have been suffering from negative equity due to the property slump since the Asian economic crisis."[9]

Social disharmony aside, another noxious effect of economic concentration is a shriveling economy. As conglomerates take more slices of the economic pie through incessant acquisitions, there are naturally fewer left for small and medium entrepreneurs outside of the power ring. Even within the limited scope of business opportunities, survival rate for small and medium enterprises is not high. These enterprises have been for a long time operating in hardship due to the high cost environment. Adding to that hardship is their relative financial vulnerability when their businesses reach an optimum stage of expansion. They are easily made victims of rent escalation at such juncture, which often works to chip away at their profit margins and eventually lead to their demise in some cases.

In other cases, their inability to compete with powerful conglomerates in terms of product pricing, like in the case of grocery stores competing with the supermarket chains, is a major cause for their extinction. As more of these enterprises get elbowed out of the market, there are fewer employers in the economy, which means lesser job opportunities for workers. At the end of the day, the whole economy will likely become stifled by concentration and the economic pie will only shrink in size.

More often than not, owners of super economic and financial power are likely to use that power in a political way to advance their interests further. With the use of such political influence, the powerhouses are often able to sway public policies in their favor, while jeopardizing the interests of the social majority.

As reported in an *Asiaweek* article, an alleged interesting incident that illustrated the kind of political influence the super-rich had over government took place in late 1998. The property market collapse earlier that year and developers' plea for action had prompted government to suspend land sales in July for the rest of that fiscal year. In his policy speech in October 1998, Tung pledged a review in early 1999 on whether to resume land sales, rather than suspend them for another two years as the Real Estate Developers' Association had wanted. Having already been dismayed at Tung's "85,000 policy" in 1997, some tycoons found it unbearable that Tung was recalcitrant towards their demands. Tung had his reasons for wanting to resume land sales in April 1999, as he had to grapple with a ballooning budget deficit, which was estimated by some analysts to reach US$832 million by March 1999.[10]

Rumors ran that the tycoons complained to the central government in Beijing and Tung was said to have asked China to help convince developers that land sales must resume. Their deadlock would not be broken were it not for former Premier Zhu Rongji's arbitrating efforts. Zhu happened to be traveling to Guangdong in late October to inspect the province's anti-smuggling and financial restructuring efforts. He spent two days in Shantou, where he met with ten Hong Kong tycoons one by one, including Li Ka-shing, Walter Kwok, Lee Shau-kee and Cheng Yu-tung. Zhu asked the magnates to try to understand Tung's difficult position and to consider Hong Kong's interests as a whole when making commercial decisions. He urged them to back the resumption of land sales in April. On his return from Shantou, Li took the lead in publicly reversing his previous opposition to restarting land sales. REDA president Stanley Ho, who obviously was not present at the Shantou meeting, complained that Li was breaking a consensus reached during a REDA meeting.

REDA is the most high-profile pressure group to date, with membership consisting of representatives from all property blue-chip companies. Members include chief executives/top managers from listed developers Cheung Kong Holdings, Sun Hung Kai Properties, Henderson Land, Swire Pacific, Wharf/Wheelock group, New World Development, Hang Lung Properties, Sino Land, Hopewell Holdings, Hysan Development, Great Eagle and Shun Tak group. The incumbent president is Macau casino magnate Stanley Ho, whose shipping group Shun Tak diversified into the business of property development in Hong Kong.

In another instance, REDA used its muscle to influence the legislation process of the new Town Planning Bill. It was stated as one of the key objectives of the new bill to make the planning system more open and accountable to the public. However, this was not what developers wanted. In a letter dated November 26, 1999 to Gordon Siu, former Secretary for

Planning, Environment and Lands, REDA made this representation under the heading "Public Comment on Planning Applications":

"The proposed public notification of development applications remains a matter of concern. Government has proposed that a list of selected uses be published to limit those applications which require public notification. As there is no indication of the type of use or basis upon which this list will be drawn up, there would appear to be no opportunity to object to the uses on the list. As this notification requirement will inevitably delay the development process and result in disclosure of the applicant's information which is currently correctly treated as being private, we believe the list should be restricted to exceptional cases...... It may also increase the public's anticipation of a greater say in the private development process to a level greater than the law could reasonably provide, creating public frustration with the whole process. In turn, this may result in public intervention and protests, beyond the level currently envisaged as being reasonable. We therefore consider this whole notification process one which needs to be handled with great care, or possibly excluded."

Then the new bill proceeded to the Committee stage in the Legislative Council. A Bills Committee was formed in early March 2000 to consider the Bill and the public submissions on the Bill. REDA's 19-page formal submission was made on March 21, 2000, in which it reiterated its comment on "Public Participation in Planning Application (Section 34)":

"It is government's view that in the existing planning system there are insufficient mechanisms for public participation. In order to address this issue, government has proposed public consultation in planning study and plan making stages and that a list of selected uses be published to prescribe those applications which require public notification. REDA fully supports the proposal for public consultation at the planning study and plan making stages. This will enable the public's views to be considered and addressed in the early stage. REDA has great concern however over the proposed public notification and comment of certain prescribed development applications, without knowing the proposed uses that will be subject to public notification. As this notification and comment requirement will inevitably delay the development process and result in disclosure of the applicant's information which is currently treated as private, we believe that the list should be restricted to exceptional cases such as offensive uses."

The Committee was not able to complete consideration of the Bill within the last term of the Legislative Council and was dissolved in May 2000. Since then the Housing, Planning and Lands Bureau decided that views on certain complex policy issues were so diverse that they needed to be resolved after further consultation with the main stakeholders. As a result, the Bureau saw benefits in putting forward an Amendment Bill that focused on improving the efficiency and effectiveness of the present planning system (which is favorable to developers), while deferring other proposed amendments to a later stage. In effect, the Bureau put aside amendments that were related to public accountability. The Amendment Bill was in reality a watered down version of the original new bill.

Economic powerhouses sometimes exert their political influence through their allies who occupy key positions at major institutions. As an international financial center, Hong Kong has a vested interest in the efficient, fair, and effective regulation of her securities and futures markets. Yet an incident again shows that private business interests are better served than those of the public.

Since the "penny stocks" incident[11] in the second half of 2002, the then Financial Secretary called in a three-member Expert Group to review the regulatory structure and make recommendations for reform. The Group released its report on March 21, 2003 calling for significant reform to be carried out urgently in the interest of maintaining Hong Kong's credibility as a leading international financial center in the Asia Pacific region. The axis of the report was in the recommendation to remove the listing function from HKEx, a listed company made up of members of the Stock and Futures Exchanges, and to vest it in the Securities and Futures Commission (SFC). Indeed, the present structure where HKEx, itself a listed company motivated by profitability, also assumes the regulatory role, was criticized by the Expert Group as "fundamentally flawed".[12]

An intriguing incident arose when, Charles Lee Yeh-kwong, former chairman of HKEx, having indicated on March 24 (in a meeting with pro-reform commentator David Webb) the company's support of the Group's recommendations and willingness to co-operate with government, made an about-turn four days later by writing to the Secretary for Financial Services to voice HKEx's opposition to the proposals. As a result, the Financial Secretary declared that the Expert Group's report would be shelved for one year, pending results of wider public consultation on the issue.

In Webb's article entitled "Disserving the Public Interest" dated March 31, 2003, he made this remark:

"Whether or not the government's commitment to implement the report's recommendations is followed through is ultimately in the hands of Mr. Tung Chee-hwa, chief executive of Hong Kong, and will be evident from his actions in the next two weeks." He further said: "Currently, 8 out of 15 directors are appointed by the government, including the chairman of HKEx who is subject to approval of the chief executive of Hong Kong. This will be reduced to 6 out of 13 after the AGM, the balance being 6 elected directors and the chief executive of HKEx, who is subject to approval by the SFC after consulting the Financial Secretary. The government has yet to announce who those 6 appointed directors will be (including the chairman), so now more than ever, government has the power to decide whether the appointed directors (and also the chief executive) are pro-reform or anti-reform. Those who are anti-reform, including Mr. Lee, need not be re-appointed, but if they are, then we will know for sure which camp Mr. Tung sits in. His government's choice of directors, chairman and chief executive will be litmus test of whether he favors the vested interests of tycoons or the long-term interests of Hong Kong as a financial center."[13]

On April 15, 2003 HKEx held its AGM and the government-appointed directors and chairman were named. Apart from one newcomer, who is a consultant with a leading accounting firm, the remaining five were re-appointments, including Lee as chairman of HKEx and former Growth Enterprise Market (GEM) chairman Lo Ka-shui as director. But the catch was, Webb plus two others who Webb believed were in the pro-reform camp, were elected directors. Another consolation was, Lee, Lo and one other re-appointed director were only given a one-year term while the remaining three were given a two-year term. Still, it looked like Webb would have one uphill battle to fight on the reform front as the new board was still dominated by vested interests. It is also a known fact that Lee's and Lo's connections with local tycoons are notably profound.

From a reasonable man's viewpoint, government's hesitation in pushing through the reform proposals was at least as much a conundrum as Lee's about-turn, if not more. The Expert Group's report was, in Webb's words, "thoughtful, deliberative, almost comprehensive and certainly far reaching". Two major issues touched on by the Expert Group were the quality of market and conflict of interests, which were truly matters of great concern to the investment community and the public alike. Not only were the study results and analysis fair and objective, but the Group's recommendations on how best to solve the present problems faced by HKEx were also logical and rational. However, such issues were nonentities when compared to the interests of the gigantic business groups. Keeping the listing function within the domain of HKEx under Lee's chairmanship would at least be helpful to the powerhouses, in case they needed listing approval for the future spin-offs of their business units.

Chapter 6

Possible Solutions

"Only I can change my life.
No one can do it for me."

– *Carol Burnett*

Perhaps no one can ever claim to have a panacea for all the social and economic ills that Hong Kong is now facing. That said, indisputable is the fact that she needs urgent treatment if she is ever to recover from those ills. In general, most of her ills are related to land and property and are all manifest in the high cost environment. Land and spatial monopolization by developer conglomerates, made possible by the historic and current operation of the land system (including an implicit high land price policy), has been the fundamental underlying cause for that environment. The workings of the land system, both historic and current, one that focuses on supply restriction and gives a comparative land cost advantage to key players, have been responsible for encouraging that monopolization to continue. Thus, possible cure could be in the form of major reforms to the land system and changes in government's land and housing policies that could reverse the high cost situation as well as mitigate the harmful effects of land and spatial monopolization by conglomerates.

In general, government has to convince itself that there are benefits in pursuing a low land price policy, not the least of which is Hong Kong regaining cost competitiveness relative to neighboring countries and mainland cities, enabling her to attract foreign investments. Other benefits include lower living costs and increased business and job opportunities for Hong Kong people, as the costs of doing business become more reasonable and affordable. Government has first to admit that the economy has been stifled out of vitality by an uncompetitive business environment and abnormally high living and business costs.

Far from deserving the accolade that Hong Kong is the freest economy in the world, she has in reality been restrained from achieving free market goals, namely, those of promoting competition and consumers' interests, of maintaining a level playing field in all business sectors and of nurturing fairness and equal opportunities for all. Through lack of a competition law and a statutory body for its enforcement, and the prevalence of monopolies and oligopolies in key economic sectors, Hong Kong is far from meeting the criteria of a truly free economy.

Concomitantly, her society suffers social injustice, either as consumers in terms of paying unfair prices, lack of product choice and bargaining power, or as small and new market players in terms of an uneven playing field and high entry barriers, or as job seekers in terms of reduced employment opportunities as a result of industrial and economic concentration. Unequivocally, a partial solution to this problem lies in the introduction without further delay of a comprehensive competition policy and consumer protection policy, and the promulgation of relevant laws.

To address the social ill of phenomenal wealth disparity, which has stemmed from the land system, being the main underlying cause for industrial and economic concentration, the present taxation structure warrants a thorough review with an aim to reforming it based on the principle that those who are more capable should bear the bigger tax burden. Any effort in narrowing the existing abysmal wealth gap, including the wide income gap amongst salaried workers, would be in the interests of social justice. The existing pro-rich taxation system has been partly responsible for stretching the already wide rich-poor gap farther apart. Besides, the poor majority as represented by the working class have always been in a disadvantaged position vis a vis employers, especially large corporations, because of outdated labor laws that are out of step with Hong Kong's economic development. To protect workers from exploitation by employers, setting a statutory minimum wage rate and legalizing workers' collective bargaining rights would be a bare minimum that government could do in this respect.

To counter the uneven wealth distributing effect that land monopoly has on society, there is a hypothetical solution that is worth intellectual debate and in-depth study. The solution calls for what social reformers refer to as "land value taxation". The notion of a land value tax is at least a hundred years old but has recently found favor again with social reformers in western countries like the U.S. and the U.K. Irrespective of whether concrete application is viable for Hong Kong, the concept is certainly a sound and logical one and at least deserves discussion amongst scholars and politicians.

ATTACKING THE PROBLEM AT ITS CORE

Why has Hong Kong remained one of the most expensive places to live and do business in? An obvious answer would seem to be scarcity of usable land. But this scarcity is in fact more of a function of government applying artificial restriction to supply, than in actuality. The land system in Hong Kong is one that focuses on supply restriction and the resulting artificial land shortage has been conducive to the pervasive high cost setting. At the same time, land and spatial monopolization by a few conglomerates, which contributes to an uncompetitive market structure, has enabled the oligarchy to exercise market power and keep property prices and rents artificially inflated. This has been one major obstacle in the downward adjustment process of property prices and rents (especially retail rents, which affect retail goods and services prices) during the 1998-2003 down cycle.

In retrospect, deliberate restriction of land supply, coupled with land monopoly and market dominance by the developer conglomerates, was at least partly instrumental in creating the early- to mid-1990s property bubble, which was bloated further by frenzied speculation. Bearing in mind that property prices had gone up five- to six-fold in the six years from 1991, a 65 per cent correction from the 1997 peak could hardly be called drastic, not to mention that the price loss began to be reversed by 2004. Although residential rents more or less moved downwards in tandem with residential prices in the "down years", retail rents on the other hand, especially those at conglomerate-owned large shopping centers, showed much more resilience by comparison.

As such, property prices and rents in general are still at a historically high level, and they contribute to the high living and business costs here. It would therefore appear that a great part of Hong Kong's high-cost problems lies in land monopoly and the distorted property market structure, made possible by the workings of the land system.

To address the high cost problems in Hong Kong and the underlying land monopoly and property market structure distortion, one practical and direct method would be for government to employ a low land price policy through the release of abundant land supplies, with allocation primarily targeted at affordable housing and economic restructuring needs.

If land costs are kept at a constant low level, the noxious effect of land and spatial monopolization by conglomerates could at least be mitigated or partially countered. High land costs resulting from artificial supply restriction have been a key contributing factor to the high business and living costs in Hong Kong and hence a major stumbling block to her regaining competitiveness. Deliberately adopting low land prices in affordable housing and restructuring-related areas would serve to anchor land prices in general at a lower level, and in turn, lower land prices would hopefully exert a natural gravitating pressure on property prices and rents. For all this to happen, government has to, in the first place, voluntarily accept that a low land price policy is the right medicine to heal Hong Kong of her socio-economic sicknesses that have chiefly arisen from an inherently unfair land system and flawed land policies.

Suspension of the HOS may be viewed as a good measure by government and the developer conglomerates, but a bad one from the angle of the lower-income group who have limited means for their housing needs. The measure no doubt answered well government's quest to cut public spending and to curb its intervention in the property market in the early 2000s. It also suited the developers well as it would mean less competition and hence even more market power. But what about the less privileged members of society who have a need to improve their living conditions but nevertheless cannot afford to buy or rent in the private housing market? It would only be socially fair, after all, for any citizen to claim his/her entitlement to decent affordable housing in a society with a government as affluent as that in Hong Kong.

As the Citizens Party (an interest group) points out in its submission paper entitled "A New Direction for Public Housing in Hong Kong", government should ensure that land would not be a deterrent in the supply of housing while the demand and supply of housing should be left to the workings of market forces. While market forces could be allowed to play out in the private housing market, which chiefly caters to the middle- to high-income group, government should not neglect the housing needs of the lower-income class on the other hand.[1]

The former Secretary for Housing, Planning and Lands pledged, in his 2003 Policy Agenda, to ensure a sufficient supply of land to meet market demand, saying "we would put in place a comprehensive monitoring mechanism and an early warning system to ensure the timely provision of land for residential development", but he stopped short of mentioning any land allocation plan aimed at providing affordable housing.

It is understandable that government no longer wants to be a developer of subsidized homes, but it cannot just walk away from the deprived social group who used to rely on the HOS for their housing needs. Why not let the private developers fill this role that government has vacated? All government has to do is to allocate land for this specific purpose and the rest could be carried out by developers. In order to ensure affordability of such type of housing, a special clause limiting the sales price or rent (or specifying a certain percentage discount to market price or rent) could be written into the Conditions of Sale (the arrangement would be similar to the Private Sector Participation Scheme, "PSPS").

To increase flexibility, developers could be allowed to retain the flats for rental purpose. Government could continue its former role under the HOS as the adjudicator of income qualifications of applicants for such flats. Not only would this measure prevent the situation where developers could amass further market power through the demand shift from public housing to the private market, it would at the same time avoid depriving the sandwich and low-income class of their basic social right – a right to a decent abode at an affordable price or rent.

Apart from affordable housing, government's long-term land allocation plan should be orientated towards economic restructuring. It would be logical to consider land allocation in light of land use needs that arise from any industrial innovation. A certain degree of open-mindedness and flexibility on the part of the authorities is not only desirable but highly necessary. Such an approach should apply not only to the usage of new lands, but also to conversion of existing use into a desired use when such applications are made.

Economist Steven Cheung Ng-sheong once wrote articles recommending the conversion of deserted flatted factories in industrial areas into trade-related exhibition halls for the purpose of promoting trade exhibitions, both of mainland-made goods and of foreign-made goods. Products to be exhibited could range from furniture, ready-to-wear clothing, electric appliances, lightings, to toys, utensils etc. The idea was to encourage foreign traders to display their goods as well as purchase China-made products that are on display at these exhibitions, while at the same time letting mainland enterprises display their products and develop overseas markets through making contacts at the exhibitions. Both wholesale and retail activities could be promoted at these exhibitions.

However, one problem with Cheung's proposal is that those factories are privately owned and any change of use would have to be voluntarily initiated by the owner(s). In cases where the factories are strata-titled, change of existing use would obviously be much more complicated. But his idea of attracting mainland as well as international traders to trade exhibitions in Hong Kong was certainly an irresistible one and one which warranted serious consideration by concerned parties, especially officials at the Housing, Planning and Lands Bureau on the issue of land allocation for this particular purpose. For Cheung's suggestion to be viable, one prerequisite would be competitive land cost, because Hong Kong would be facing one tough competitor in this arena, and that is Shanghai, where both land and labor costs are cheaper than Hong Kong, according to the economist.

If after careful studies it is found that Cheung's idea is workable, then let it not be hampered by rigidity and bureaucratic red tape on government's part. It would make sense to provide, preferably at nominal cost, suitably zoned and accessible sites for this specified use. Only with very low land cost could the rent for such trade exhibition facilities be set at a sufficiently competitive level relative to Shanghai. The long-term economic and social benefits to be reaped from trade activities and their multiplying effects should probably be sufficient to offset the short-term loss in land revenue. After all, what better role can Hong Kong play than providing window-display support with superb infrastructure facilities to the world's largest factory? In the process, much needed employment would be created as businesses start flowing through Hong Kong. Trade exhibition facilities with affordable rent would also be welcomed by those self-employed who have a need to use such facilities to display their works, e.g. local artists, local designers etc. To safeguard against developer conglomerates devouring cheap lands for such use, again a price or rent cap clause should be written in the new land grants.

Where land supply for private residential (other than affordable housing) and commercial and industrial uses (apart from economic restructuring-related needs) is concerned, the basic principle to follow would be to allow as much competition as possible by the consistent generous release of land with a crystal clear message to the market that no land supply shortage would ever occur. To allow market forces to take hold in the private residential and commercial land market, it would be advisable to resume public land auction as soon as possible. Also, to encourage smaller, less well-capitalized, players to compete for sites put up at auctions, government could consider offering more small-sized lots for public sale and introducing a payment-by-instalments method for the payment of land premium.

Consumers in the private residential market often make uninformed home purchase decisions as useful and relevant data is simply not available to them. To increase market transparency, the Housing Bureau could make public its annual projections of population growth, demographic changes and income distribution plus all data relevant to housing demand, while the Planning and Lands Bureau could announce regularly its long-term land disposal programs. It would obviously be desirable for these Bureaus to share their projections and data with the public so that the latter can make informed decisions when considering a home purchase, which in most cases is the single largest investment of one's lifetime. Better-informed consumers would be more price-conscious and be less likely objects of exploitation.

Contributing to the distorted land and property market structure has been the conglomerates' land cost edge through the workings of the lease modification system and their owning huge agricultural and utility or public service land reserves. While the lease modification system may well be a flexible system that allows landowners to apply for conversion of land use for their lands, the fact that modification premium valuation details are never disclosed certainly raises the question of public accountability, as such premiums form a big portion of government's total land revenue. The public should at least be informed as to how those premiums are calculated. This apart, exploitation of land assets of utility or public bus companies by their controlling conglomerates through lease modification should be a subject for examination in relation to social fairness, as those land assets were granted for public purpose in the first place and should not be used for private purpose at will. To prevent future exploitation of such assets, government could consider inserting a land resumption clause in the lease for future land grants.

Land monopoly is not by any means a new socio-economic problem. Less than a hundred years ago, in a speech to the House of Commons in 1909, Winston Churchill clearly spelled out the evils of land monopoly. Here is an excerpt of that speech:

"Land monopoly is not the only monopoly, but it is by far the greatest of monopolies – it is a perpetual monopoly, and it is the mother of all other forms of monopoly. Unearned increments in land are not the only form of unearned or undeserved profit, but they are the principal form of unearned increment, and they are derived from processes which are not merely not beneficial, but positively detrimental to the general public.

Land, which is a necessity of human existence, which is the original source of all wealth, which is strictly limited in extent, which is fixed in geographical position – land, I say, differs from all other forms of property. ......Nothing is more amusing than to watch the efforts of land monopolists to claim that other forms of property and increment are similar in all respects to land and the unearned increment on land. They talk of the increased profits of a doctor or lawyer from the growth of population in the town in which they live. ......They talk of the profits from a rise in stocks and even the profits derived from the sale of works of art. ......

If a rise in stocks confers profits on the fortunate holders far beyond what they expected or indeed deserved, nevertheless that profit was not reaped by withholding from the community the land which it needs; on the contrary, it was reaped by supplying industry with the capital without which it could not be carried on. ......If a doctor or a lawyer enjoys a better practice, it is because the doctor attends more patients and more exacting patients, and because the lawyer pleads more suits in the courts and more important suits. At every stage the doctor or the lawyer is giving service in return for his fees.

Fancy comparing these healthy processes with the enrichment which comes to the landlord who happens to own a plot of land on the outskirts of a great city, who watches the busy population around him making the city larger, richer, more convenient, more famous every day, and all the while sits still and does nothing.

Roads are made, streets are made, services are improved, electric light turns night into day, water is brought from reservoirs a hundred miles off in the mountains – and all the while the landlord sits still. Every one of those improvements is effected by the labor and cost of other people and the taxpayers. To not one of those improvements does the land monopolist, as a land monopolist, contribute, and yet by every one of them the value of his land is enhanced. He renders no service to the community, he contributes nothing to the general welfare, he contributes nothing to the process from which his own enrichment is derived. ......and all the while the land monopolist only has to sit still and watch complacently his property multiplying in value, sometimes many fold, without either effort or contribution on his part!

But let us follow this process a little further. The population of the city grows and grows, the congestion in the poorer quarters becomes acute, rents rise and thousands of families are crowded into tenements. At last the land becomes ripe for sale – that means that the price is too tempting to be resisted any longer. And then, and not until then, it is sold by the yard or by the inch at 10 times, or 20 times, or even 50 times its agricultural value.

The greater the population around the land, the greater the injury the public has sustained by its protracted denial. And, the more inconvenience caused to everybody, the more serious the loss in economic strength and activity – the larger will be the profit of the landlord when the sale is finally accomplished. ......It is monopoly which is the keynote, and where monopoly prevails, the greater the injury to society, the greater the reward to the monopolist. This evil process strikes at every form of industrial activity. ......

No matter where you look or what examples you select, you will see every form of enterprise, every step in material progress, is only undertaken after the land monopolist has skimmed the cream for himself, and everywhere today the man or the public body that wishes to put land to its highest use is forced to pay a preliminary fine in land values to the man who is putting it to an inferior one, and in some cases to no use at all. All comes back to land value, and its owner is able to levy toll upon all other forms of wealth and every form of industry. A portion, in some cases the whole, of every benefit which is laboriously acquired by the community increases the land value and finds its way automatically into the landlord's pocket. If there is a rise in wages, rents are able to move forward, because the workers can afford to pay a little more. If the opening of a new railway or new tramway, or the institution of improved services of a lowering of fares, or of a new invention, or any other public convenience affords a benefit to workers in any particular district, it becomes easier for them to live, and therefore the ground landlord is able to charge them more for the privilege of living there ......

All goes back to the land, and the landowner is able to absorb to himself a share of almost every public and every private benefit, however important or however pitiful those benefits may be. ......"

What is striking about the speech is that the description of how a landlord benefits from just hanging on to a piece of land (mostly for agricultural use) for years and then reaping all the public benefits accrued to it, bears so much resemblance to a prevailing process whereby a Hong Kong developer profits from owning a piece of agricultural land in Hong Kong and then ultimately developing it for lucrative residential use when the opportunity is ripe (e.g. when a new railway is put in operation or when a new town is inaugurated). The sad thing is, what was viewed as undesirable so many years ago is still in practice today and causing a lot of social problems.

At the end of his speech, Churchill emphasized that it was not the individual landowner who was at fault. Rather, it was the system that should be blamed. "It is not the man who is bad; it is the law which is bad. It is not the man who is blameworthy for doing what the law allows and what other men do; it is the State which would be blameworthy if it were not to endeavor to reform the law and correct the practice," he said. Indeed, in Hong Kong's present situation, it would be government, rather than the developer conglomerates, who ought to be blamed if it does not attempt to take remedial actions to rectify the problems brought about by the land and tax systems in combination.

ANTI-CONCENTRATION AND CONSUMER PROTECTION

Competition policy is increasingly acknowledged as a tool that promotes economic development as evidenced by the increasing number of countries that enact and enforce competition laws. The focus of competition law and policy is the market-dominating behavior of businesses through, inter alia, price fixing or market-sharing cartels, abuses by leading firms and anti-competitive mergers and acquisitions. The main objective of such a policy and law is to promote competition as a means of creating markets that are responsive to consumer demands, of efficient allocation of resources in the economy and efficient production with innovation incentives. The result would be the best possible choice of quality, the lowest prices and sufficient supplies to consumers. Competition leads to increased competitiveness in the economy, resulting in substantial growth and development.

Evidences of monopolies and industrial concentration in various economic sectors in Hong Kong have already been dealt with in detail in previous chapters. While Hong Kong's government refused to move forward on the introduction of a comprehensive competition law, other APEC member economies have taken a more active approach. Thailand and Indonesia adopted comprehensive competition laws respectively in 1999 and 2000, while China is considering introducing such a law. Other APEC members like Taiwan, Korea and Mexico have had such laws in place for a longer time. Although Singapore has no independent comprehensive competition law, it has established competition provisions in laws regulating telecommunications, electric power and gas industries. In terms of GDP per capita, Hong Kong ranks third among the APEC members, after the U.S. and Japan. Yet she is one of the few left who have yet to catch up with global practices on the competition issue.

In a submission paper to the 2002 APEC Workshop on Competition Policy and Deregulation, host country Mexico lists out three negative effects of a monopoly:

"On one hand, a monopoly can obtain extraordinary rents by reducing output and increasing prices, thereby having the effect of redistributing income from consumers to producers. On the other hand, this distortion in the allocation of resources brings about a once and for all reduction of the domestic product available for distribution among the country's population (net social welfare loss). The third negative effect of a monopoly derives from the existing incentives to capture the extra normal rents the monopoly generates. The firm's managers, workers and providers try to get hold of higher salaries and conditions than those that would prevail under competitive conditions. This situation leads to an undesirable result that the firm produces at inefficient costs and society incurs a net welfare loss because the costs of production are higher than those that would prevail under competitive conditions."

The paper also says that when a market is in the form of a cartel, the resulting inefficiencies and distortions are the same as those in a monopoly. A cartel exists when competitors engage in horizontal agreements to fix prices, restrict output, allocate markets or rig bids. It is widely accepted that horizontal practices harm the economy and negatively affect its development. In Mexico, where a competition law is in place, such practices are prohibited per se.

Mexico's submission further explains how a competition policy fosters economic development in a dynamic context. The process is best analysed by the impact of such a policy on four investment decision factors, namely, income, costs, profitability and risk. A competition policy would facilitate market access by new competitors, thereby enabling the generation of productive infrastructure and income. By preventing anti-competitive practices and knocking down entry barriers, such a policy would allow new entrants to generate income in a normal business setting. The policy would also foster investments by promoting lower prices for inputs and capital goods. Growth in profitability would be a natural outcome when income increases and costs fall. Another key function of the policy would be to improve transparency of the game rules for investors, and thus it would help to reduce investment risks. In short, competition works as a fuel for economic vitality. A monopolized market lacking contestability would unlikely result in continuous improvement and innovation, since the monopolist, facing no rivals, has no incentives to satisfy its captive consumers. In conclusion, Mexico asserts that its experience in the enforcement of competition law demonstrates that competition is a powerful tool for the promotion of economic development.[2]

In an Expert Meeting of United Nations Conference on Trade and Development (UNCTAD) held in Geneva in October 2001, it was noted that it would not be sufficient merely to adopt competition legislation: economies still had to be able to enforce it properly. Examples were cited of authorities lacking resources to investigate complaints, and of large firms able to exert political influence against decisions providing relief. It was recognized that consumers in developing countries suffered most from market distortions and asymmetry of information. Thus there was a need to adopt consumer protection legislation. At the same time consumer education efforts were also needed, especially to inform low-income consumers about their rights and duties. It was pointed out that competition laws and consumer protection shared the same goals, namely, the defence of consumer interests, but that the two were considered to be complementary. While effective competition policy could benefit consumers indirectly, consumer protection rules were necessary in order to take care of consumers' immediate concerns. For example, consumers were easy targets for unscrupulous sellers cheating on weights and measures, quality standards, and so forth, as well as misrepresentations and misleading advertising.

There is obviously as much a need in Hong Kong as in developing countries to adopt consumer protection legislation. To cite one example, consumers in the property market have long suffered from lack of consumer protection. One major problem lies in the confusing measurement terms used in various documents and the varied interpretation of those terms. For example, some developers would list both "saleable floor area" and "gross floor area" of a flat in a sales brochure, while some would only list "gross floor area". While the unit price is based on "gross floor area", the sales and purchase agreement, which is a legally binding document, only mentions the "saleable floor area", which measurement is the only standardized measurement in the industry based on the definition by the Hong Kong Institute of Surveyors. "Buildable gross floor area" as defined in the Conditions of Sale for public land auctions or tenders, on which the land premium is based, does not match, in terms of total measurement, the "gross floor area" which appears in a flat sales brochure (i.e. the latter measurement is a much inflated figure).

Then there is either the exclusion or inclusion of "bay window" area from or within the "gross floor area" in the sales brochure. "Gross floor area" as it appears in a sales brochure usually includes the area within the four walls of a flat plus an apportionment of common areas (including clubhouse and carpark areas in some cases) outside of the flat. Even in the apportioning of common areas, one developer may follow one set of rules while another may have a different set. In some cases, a buyer gets an efficiency ratio of only about 70 per cent in terms of usable area relative to "gross floor area", on which the unit price is based. Despite frequent calls on government to standardize measurements of flats for sale with an aim to prevent fraudulent practices, nothing concrete has so far been implemented. Moreover, buyers do not have a cooling off period in new flat purchase transactions. Nor are they protected by any kind of building warranty for an investment that would cost them a big chunk of their lifetime earnings.

The UNCTAD Expert Meeting noted that properly implemented competition and consumer protection policies could make a key contribution to competitiveness and development of an economy, especially those in developing countries. The meeting noted that market failures posed major challenges to consumers, in that consumers could be easily misled by all sorts of unfair or fraudulent business practices, such as misleading advertising and the sale of substandard goods and services. In some cases, privatization and deregulation had taken place with scant regard for consumer interests, and often in the absence of legal and institutional frameworks for consumer protection.

The experts proposed that governments take the necessary steps to implement the UN Guidelines for Consumer Protection, as extended in 1999 to cover sustained consumption. Governments should develop and maintain competition and consumer protection policies and laws which were mutually reinforcing, with a view to promoting competitive markets, consumer welfare, competitiveness and development. It was proposed that consumer interests be better taken into account at all decision-making levels in government and that specific channels and mechanisms be created in this respect. Special emphasis was placed on the need to encourage consumer information and education programs. Enterprises were advised to conform with relevant laws and regulations and with the UN Set of Multilaterally Agreed Equitable Principles and Rules for the Control of Restrictive Business Practices. Consumer associations were called on to develop regional training and information programs for consumers in cooperation with government, business, international organizations and academia.[3]

As an advanced economy in terms of GDP per capita on the world stage, Hong Kong has little reason to delay any longer the introduction of comprehensive competition and consumer protection policies and laws, particularly in light of the weak position her consumers are in relevant to overbearing conglomerates. Traditionally, competition law deals with issues that fall under three broad categories: (1) monopoly or abuse of dominance; (2) restrictive trade practices and other anti-competitive agreements; and (3) anti-competitive mergers and acquisitions.[4] Naturally, such a law would be subject to adaptation depending on Hong Kong's own needs, aspirations and socio-economic, cultural and legal conditions.

For law enforcement, a competition authority with powers resembling those of the European Commission would be an option. Like the Commission, the authority would have considerable powers to investigate suspected abuses of competition law. The rights of the parties under investigation would be guaranteed, as would their commercial confidentiality. Competition policy would be ineffective if the authority's monitoring and control activities were not accompanied by decisions and penalties. Thus, the authority should be given considerable powers to prohibit anti-competitive activities, to issue injunctions against, and to impose fines on firms found guilty of anti-competitive conduct.[5]

As a check on the absolute power of the proposed competition authority, it may be advisable to keep investigative and adjudicative functions separate. Also, the competition authority would probably have a direct overlap with regulators governing utility sectors, e.g. Office of the Telecommunications Authority. Ideally, the utility regulators should concentrate on tariffs and the setting of performance standards, while the competition authority would deal with the abuse of dominance and other anti-competitive practices when they arise. In any case, the competition authority should have overriding power on competition matters, as utility regulators are more closely connected with business groups in their industry and may not be totally objective in judgment.

As regards Hong Kong's utility monopolies (electricity and gas), perhaps reference could be drawn from the European Commission's approach of separating infrastructure from commercial activities. In the

Commission's view, monopolies have been in network industries like transport, energy and telecommunications. In these sectors, a distinction must be made between the infrastructure and the services provided over this infrastructure. While it is often difficult to establish a second, competing infrastructure, for reasons linked to investment costs and economic efficiency, it is possible and desirable to create competitive conditions in respect of the services provided. The Commission has therefore developed the concept of separating infrastructure from commercial activities. While the right to exclusive ownership may persist as regards the infrastructure (the telephone or electricity network for example), monopolists must grant access to companies wishing to compete with them as regards the services offered on their networks. This is the general principle on which the European Union's liberalization directives are based. The European Union has introduced directives to initiate the opening up of these markets: telecommunications, transport, postal services, gas and electricity.[6]

A note written by the UNCTAD secretariat on August 20, 2001 says that consumer protection policy seeks to ensure that the efficiencies and innovation benefits brought about by competition are not retained by producers through misleading and deceptive conduct or unfair practices, but are instead shared with consumers. "Effective enforcement of legislation prohibiting misleading or deceptive conduct can assist the competitive process. Strong consumer protection regimes with empowered consumers can also remove managerial slackness and make firms more efficient and competitive in terms of quality and prices," the note further says. The objectives of both competition and consumer protection policies are essentially the same, but the former is more proactive in nature as it attempts to promote consumer interest in a marketplace, while the latter has a reactive approach in providing access for redress of abuses. Although Hong Kong is more advanced in terms of economic performance than most developing countries, it is obvious that her consumers have as urgent a need as those in developing countries for an effective consumer protection law and policy.

As the UNCTAD experts pointed out, education of consumers is as important as the consumer protection legislation process and this function would best be taken up by the Consumer Council with its existing establishment and resources, perhaps in conjunction with COMPAG in Hong Kong (representing government) and international organizations like UNCTAD and the APEC Competition Policy and Deregulation Group. Sectors that need special attention include property, supermarket sales, franchised bus services and other means of mass transport. Empowered consumers and representative organizations will be able to bring to the attention of the competition authority anti-competitive practices, including abuse of dominance and collusion. They will also act as a counter-balancing power to businesses to ensure effective enforcement of competition law.

Consumers also need to be included in the consultative process for policy issues. Many consumers in Hong Kong are not aware of the importance and relevance of competition policy and law. The Consumer Council has an important role here by way of education and propaganda. Unfortunately, conglomerates are better organized and financed and have acted as a strong opposing power against a legal framework for competition law and policy, which directly affect their interests. Thus, a strong and vibrant consumer movement is an important first step on the path to successful legislation, without which social inequalities and concentration of economic power in the few will continue to coexist with an increasingly inefficient marketplace, ultimately damaging Hong Kong's long-term economic outlook.

COUNTERING EXTREME WEALTH DISPARITY

Eradication of poverty and social equality is the ultimate ideology of any free economy. Finland is one country that has nothing but success to show for her strife for that goal. Based on UN statistics, Finland is the most equal society in the world, with regard to both class and gender, and open poverty and misery are almost non-existent, according to Hikka Pietila, a scholar associated with the University of Helsinki. The following is the Finnish story, as extracted from one of her articles that appeared in the Winter 2002 issue of *YES* magazine:-:

"The common belief is that a country must first become rich, and then it can provide welfare for its people. The history of the Nordic societies tells a different story; here, wealth has been built by building welfare for people.

In the U.S., 'being on welfare' is humiliating, and welfare benefits often depend on the recipient's relationship to something or someone else. What is radically different about the Finnish system is that here welfare benefits and services are rights that everyone living permanently in the country is individually entitled to. ......

The social progress in Finland in the early 1900s proves that empowering women and strengthening their competence to help themselves is the way to eradicate poverty. It is social policy from below, building self-reliant and sustainable well-being for the whole nation. This progress paved the way for the creation of the welfare system after World War II. Finland was not a wealthy country in the 1940s and 1950s. ......

Despite its poverty, Finland began to create one of the world's most generous social welfare systems. The aim was to build the economy while eradicating poverty. The aims supported each other: the growing well-being of people provided a healthy and well-trained labor force, and the economic growth was redistributed to people as social benefits.

As Finland's economy grew, the welfare system grew, so that today, everyone is entitled to a minimum salary or unemployment benefit, child-support allowances for all children, paid parental leave for 11 weeks, pensions, free education up to university level, free school meals to all pupils in public comprehensive schools, highly subsidized public health services, day care services for all children under school age and subsidized care for the aged.

The government also provides good public transport, free universities in 10 cities around the country, high-quality public primary and secondary schools and vocational training, a comprehensive adult education system, excellent public libraries all over the country, and highly subsidized theatre, music and arts in all cities. The welfare system here is a lifelong social insurance, a guarantee that whatever may happen, children will not lose access to education, people will not be left at the mercy of relatives or charity organizations, no one will be abandoned in case of illnesses, accidents, unemployment, or bankruptcy, and everyone will have old-age income and care no matter what. Open poverty and misery are almost nonexistent."[7]

Doesn't that sound paradise on earth? Wouldn't the majority of Hong Kong people dream that one day they would enjoy the same welfare benefits the Finns do? Of course, sweet as the story may sound, there is in reality no free lunch in this world. The catch is that Finland has financed its welfare system mainly through highly progressive taxation on salaries and wages. Taxes can be as high as 50 to 60 per cent of salaries and wages for those who earn the most. Yet their people have gladly accepted such a tax system in a socially responsible way.

It has often been argued that Hong Kong owes its economic advancement to her simple tax structure with low tax rates, which should thus be kept unchanged. While there is every truth in that premise in the early stages of development in her economy, the success she has achieved over the years has thrown a different light on the logic of maintaining that status quo. She is now considered a rich economy in terms of her GDP per capita, but paradoxically a surprisingly large proportion of her population still live below the poverty line. It is also apparent that her income gap has polarized to an alarming extent as she enjoyed rapid economic growth over the past few decades.

According to the Taxation Institute of Hong Kong, Hong Kong's direct tax system (on both corporate and personal income) adopts a combination of proportional (standard rates for corporate and individual are 16.5 and 15 per cent respectively) and progressive rates, which are considered low relative to other tax jurisdictions that support substantive operations. The long-applauded low rate and simple tax structure has certainly contributed to her success story, but, on the flip side of the coin, has also been an indirect cause of her worsening wealth disparity.

If any relief is ever to be forthcoming, a drastic overhaul of the present taxation structure and underlying principles and philosophy is a must. The axle question to ask is: do Hong Kong people aspire to have a society modeled after Finland, one in which there is social equality and no poverty and misery? If the answer is positive, then one of the most important areas to look into is the present tax regime. To be included in the agenda for change may be a more highly progressive salaries tax rate and the introduction of other taxes targeted at the upper echelons of society, like a wealth tax, capital gains tax and dividends tax etc. A highly progressive tax means that the "last" dollar of income earned is subject to increasingly higher marginal tax rates as income increases. In other words, the average tax rate rises with income, causing taxpayers with higher taxable income to pay a proportionately larger share of their income in taxes than those with lower income.

The most compelling reason for the rich-targeted taxes, especially a wealth tax, is equity. Taxes should be levied on the basis of the ability to pay. Income alone is not an adequate gauge of personal or family net worth or of taxable capacity. The possession of wealth adds to this capacity, over and above the income it yields. Wealth gives a family greater ability to pay taxes, and in the interests of equity, it is fair to tax current wealth in addition to income. Countries that have a wealth tax in place include Austria, Denmark, Finland, Germany, Luxembourg, the Netherlands, Norway, Sweden and Switzerland. In all cases, the wealth tax is administered in conjunction with the personal income tax.[8] Most advanced economies like the U.S. and Canada levy a capital gains tax. The net effect of the proposed changes to the current tax regime is admittedly redistributive in nature. But the proposal is conducive to achieving a less uneven distribution of income and wealth, thus promoting a more equal and fairer society. It also befits Hong Kong's present advanced phase of economic development. After all, it would only be fair for those who have taken most wealth from society to give back most in taxes.

In the interests of promoting a more equal society, furthering Hong Kong workers' welfare and rights should come second in importance after a more equitable tax regime. The struggle for collective bargaining rights and a minimum wage rate must continue despite government's reluctance to grant assent to Hong Kong Confederation of Trade Unions' (HKCTU) demands, as these are basic human rights in a free economy.

Social reformers have long believed that to counter uneven wealth distribution brought on by land monopoly would best be solved by a unique tax system called "land value taxation". Henry George, the American reformer, founded the concept of land value taxation over a hundred years ago. It is a concept of shifting the tax burden from labor and capital to land as a solution to raising public finances efficiently and distributing wealth evenly and fairly. But whether such a system is viable for Hong Kong would be a subject for debate. Nonetheless, the concept itself seems to be a valid one and is worth in-depth study. The difficulty would mainly lie in the application as it would involve a total reform of government fiscal policies and the tax structure.

The Georgist paradigm is based on the following premise. Historically, monopoly ownership of land sites or natural resources has been the foundation of most great fortunes. Production of wealth requires three factors and these are land, labor and capital. The economic return to each of labor, capital and land are defined as wages or salaries, interest and rent respectively. Wages and interest are attributable to human effort: the laborer is rightly entitled to his wages and the owner of capital is properly entitled to the interest paid for the use of his capital. But land differs from the other two production factors in that the owner of land did not create that land or even its value. The value of land is contingent on its inherent fertility or mineral content, its location relative to population aggregation and its proximity to roads, schools and other public and commercial facilities and services.

Since the value of any parcel of land is mostly created by the community and not the individual owner of the land, the rental value of that land should be paid to the community that created that value. As such, a tax levied by the community on the market value of that land would stimulate the highest and best use of the land and promote productive employment. Such a tax increases, rather than reduces, the incentive to produce. It discourages the hoarding of land for speculative gain and increases the supply of land in the marketplace because it induces the owner to use the land efficiently or sell to those who would. Increasing the supply of land in the marketplace by increasing the tax load on land value would cause the price of land to fall and make it more affordable.

In the United States, an activist group called Common Ground – USA, whose objective is to seek social justice and economic equity for all, has published an open letter to the mayors of cities and towns in the States urging local governments to consider changing their tax regime following the principles of the Georgist paradigm.[9] The following is an extract from the open letter:

"Our research leads us to rather striking conclusions of how the way we raise our public revenue drives economic and social outcomes. What cities have to offer most is location. Cities are where they are because at some time in the past the location was advantageous: an excellent harbor, a navigable river, rich farmland, mild weather, the crossroads of natural trade routes. With the increase in population coming to live in the same geography, locations come to have exchange value. In fact, every location has some annual rental value in the marketplace. This rental value is what people are willing to give up from what they produce as payment for control over a particular location.

An important practical observation is that this location rental value grows or falls independent of what any individual does with a location. Location value is created by aggregate public and private investment. As such, this value ought to be – we would say "needs" to be – fully captured by government to pay for public goods and services. ......

A city with a low effective tax rate on location rental values will experience high levels of land hoarding and speculation, as well as land markets with a strong tendency to spiral upwards rapidly, then crash when businesses can no longer afford to absorb the higher costs of doing business triggered by the speculative land market. Strangely, we have come to accept these dynamics as the unfortunate consequences of a market economy, of the business cycle, when rational public policy could attack the problem at its core.

Our mission to provide objective and thoughtful analysis to our mayors, urging you to take the lead in removing one of the most serious impediments to the economic health of our cities by looking to location rental values as the primary source of public revenue and removing the burden of taxation from the productive activities in which we engage. Taxing (i.e. collecting) location rental values brings in revenue, discourages land speculation and pressures those who own land parcels to improve them according to the "highest and best use" as dictated by the market. When the land owner then makes an investment in a home or office building or store – improving the land parcel to its highest and best use – the best thing the city can do is exempt these assets from taxation. Exempting all property improvements from taxation simply extends this wise policy to all property owners. The same logic applies to taxes on the wages and salaries of working people and on the sales of goods. These forms of taxation started out at very low levels and have been increased over time, often in response to revenue shortfalls. The long-term impact of these measures has been to drive people and businesses to lower (or no) tax geographies.

Every city or town would benefit, we believe, by the measures we have described. Perhaps more to the point, the people who work and produce and contribute to the economic and social health of our communities will be rewarded – as they should – for doing so. Those who enjoy the privilege of controlling the use of the most desirable and potentially profitable locations in our communities will, finally, pay for this privilege."[10]

In the United Kingdom, a non-party organization called Land Value Taxation Campaign was formed to promote the adoption of land value taxation in the U.K. and to improve understanding of its economic benefits. The Campaign has provided a guideline on how land should be valued. It suggests that the value of every parcel of land in Britain would be assessed regularly and the land value tax levied as a percentage of those assessed values. "Land" for taxation purpose means the site alone, not counting any improvements. But it would be assumed that all neighboring properties were developed as at the time of the valuation; other things being equal, a vacant site in a row of houses would be assessed at the same value as the adjacent sites occupied by houses. The valuation would be based on market evidence, in accordance with the optimum use of the land within the planning regulations. If the current planning restrictions on the use were altered, the site would be reassessed.

One of the chief economic benefits that such a tax would create, the Campaign believes, is that it would avoid penalizing enterprise and efficiency through taxing labor and capital, which discourages people from constructive activities. Rather, a tax on land values is a payment, based on current market value, for the exclusive occupation of a piece of land. In the longer term, this fundamentally new approach to public revenue raising will stimulate new business and new employment, reducing the need for costly government welfare.

The Campaign stresses that it is fair to impose such a tax because "in reality land acquires a scarcity value owing to the competing needs of the community for living, working and leisure space. Thus land value owes nothing to the individual effort and everything to the community at large. It belongs justly and uniquely to the community." It says further: "Because of differences in positional advantages, fertility or natural resources, some locations are more desirable than others. Demand for access to these features gives land its rental value. Land value taxation, being assessed on these values, is fair in its incidence."[11]

As rational and fair as the land value tax idea may sound, one cannot but perceive the phenomenal attendant difficulties on its materialization, both in the political and practicality contexts. A lot more discussion and promotional effort would likely be necessary before either of the above activist groups is able to attract any significant audience in their respective countries. Any attempt to put the same message across to the Hong Kong community would only meet with much more skepticism and resistance. Still, on the level of the more enlightened, it is certainly a subject worth further looking into for the benefit of society at large.

Land has worked as an enriching agent for the ruling class in Hong Kong. Existence of such a ruling class, which thrives on land and spatial monopoly and control of other forms of economic assets, is itself a symbol that contradicts the ideals of a free economy – a state that Hong Kong is ironically believed to be in. A free economy is one where people have the opportunities to demonstrate their individual worth and where they enjoy freedom of upward social mobility. Monopolies, in particular land and spatial monopoly, on the other hand, which are the cornerstone of economic concentration, are designed to prevent an economy from operating freely and effectively, for all people and at all times. If Hong Kong is ever to have a truly free economy, one that is worthy of commendation by the international community, not only are reforms to her systems inevitable, but reforms to her society's mentalities are also a must. Any change to the present social and economic structure is clearly dependent on some kind of social consensus. That consensus would never be achievable if people approach problems from a self-interest angle rather than from a social viewpoint. For any reform to be successfully implemented, an honest, conscience-driven and socially responsible attitude on the part of government officials and members of society, one that is orientated towards social well-being, equality and fairness, is a definite prerequisite.

Notes

Prologue

1. Mercer Human Resources Consulting. 2009. *Worldwide Cost of Living Survey*
2. CB Richard Ellis' Survey (www.cbre.com)
3. Census & Statistics Department, the Government of Hong Kong Special Administrative Region
4. HOS flats are one kind of subsidized public housing in Hong Kong. The buying, selling and mortgage of these flats are subject to certain restrictions
5. Global Property Guide (www.globalpropertyguide.com))
6. For a summary of the plan, see P.25 in Chapter 1
7. Rating and Valuation Department, the Government of Hong Kong Special Administrative Region
8. Leung Chun-ying's website (www.cyleung.hk)
9. In his 1997 Policy Address, Tung Chee-hwa announced that no less than 85,000 units of residential units would be provided each year
10. The Hong Kong Housing Authority is a statutory body established to provide public housing
11. See Page 90-93 in Chapter 3
12. David Webb's website (http://webb-site.com)
13. All these were campaigns to maintain traditional buildings in local redevelopment projects

Chapter 1 : The Ruling Class

1. Hutchison Whampoa Limited website (www.hutchison-whampoa.com)
2. Feng Bangyan 馮邦彥. 1997. *Xianggang huazi caituan 1841-1997* 香港華資財團1841-1997 (Chinese Conglomerates in Hong Kong 1841-1997). Hong Kong: Joint Publishing
3. Ibid
4. *Economic Digest*. May 26, 1985. Hong Kong.
5. NWS Holdings Limited website (www.nws.com.hk)
6. CLP Group website (www.clpgroup.com.hk)
7. See Note 2
8. PCCW website (www.pccw.com.hk)
9. Hong Kong Cyberport website (www.cyberport.com.hk)
10. Reuters Business News. March 17, 2003
11. Hong Kong Exchanges & Clearing website (www.hkex.com.hk)
12. See Note 6
13. Cheung Kong Holdings website (www.ckh.com.hk)
14. Henderson Land website (www.hld.com)
15. Sun Hung Kai Properties website (www.shkp.com.hk)
16. See Note 5
17. Consumer Council. 1996. *How Competitive is the Private Residential Property Market?*
18. Cheung Kong (Holdings) 2002 Annual Report
19. Sun Hung Kai Properties 2002 Annual Report
20. Henderson Land 2002 Annual Report
21. Wharf Holdings 2002 Annual Report
22. New World Development 2002 Annual Report
23. See Note 16
24. See Note 15
25. Lam Pun-lee and Sylvia Chan. 2000. *Competition in Hong Kong's Gas Industry.* Hong Kong: The Chinese University Press
26. Consumer Council. 1995. *Assessing Competition in the Domestic Water Heating & Cooking Fuel Market.* Hong Kong
27. Lam Pun-lee. 1997. *Competition in Energy.* Hong Kong: City University of Hong Kong Press
28. Fortune website (www.fortune.com) April 4, 2002. *At PCCW, Every Old is New Again*
29. Asiaweek website (www.asiaweek.com). February 23, 2001. *Doing It Dad's Way*
30. See Note 2
31. See Note 16
32. Ibid

33. See P.70-76 in Chapter 2
34. See Note 2
35. See Note 15
36. See Note 2
37. New World Development website (www.nwd.com.hk)
38. The Wharf (Holdings) website (www.wharfholdings.com)
39. Wheelock and Company website (www.wheelockcompany.com)
40. See Note 2
41. See Note 6
42. Hongkong & Shanghai Hotels 2001 Annual Report
43. *South China Morning Post.* June 18, 2005. Hong Kong.

Chapter 2 : Land and Power

1. F. L. Ganshof. 1961 & 1964. *Feudalsim.* New York: Harper & Row
2. David Herlihy. 1970. *The History of Feudalism.* New York: Harper & Row
3. Wendy Davis and Paul Fouracre (ed). 1995. *Property and Power in the Early Middle Ages.* Cambridge: Cambridge University Press
4. R. H. Britnell. 1993. *The Commercialisation of English Society.* Cambridge: Cambridge University Press
5. Michael Hudson, G. J. Miller and Kris Feder. 1994. *A Philosophy for a Fair Society.* London: Shepheard-Walwyn
6. Fred Harrison. 1983. *The Power in the Land.* London: Shepheard-Walwyn
7. Roger Nissim. 1998. *Land Administration and Practice in Hong Kong.* Hong Kong: Hong Kong University Press
8. See Note 2 of Chapter 1
9. Ibid
10. PBS website (www.pbs.org) (on tulipmania)
11. The Dirt Gardener's website (www.dirtgardener.com) (on tulipmania)
12. See Note 17 of Chapter 1
13. The Secretary for Housing, Planning and Lands, the HKSAR government. November 13, 2002. Hong Kong
14. The HKSAR government website (ww.info.gov.hk/planning/info_serv/statistic/landu_e.htm) (Map on Land Utilization in Hong Kong 2000)

Chapter 3 : Money-Spinners vs. Public Interest

1. Past annual reports of Cheung Kong (Holdings)
2. Past annual reports of Sun Hung Kai Properties
3. Past annual reports of Henderson Land
4. Sun Hung Kai Properties website /(www.shkp.com.hk)
5. The Wharf (Holdings) website (www.wharfholdings.com)
6. Henderson Land website (www.hld.com)
7. New World Development website (www.nwd.com.hk)
8. Cheung Kong Holdings website (www.ckh.com.hk)
9. CLP Group website (www.clpgroup.com.hk)
10. Hongkong Electric Holdings website (www.hke.com.hk)
11. See Note 9
12. See Note 10
13. About Deregulation and Energy Shop website (http://www.energyshop.com/energyshop/dereg.cfm)
14. The Public Interest Advocacy Centre website (http://www.piac.ca/Ontario%20Electricity%20Restructuring1.htm)
15. See Note 27 of Chapter 1
16. Hong Kong & China Gas website (www.hkcg.com.hk)
17. Ibid
18. See Note 25 of Chapter 1
19. See Note 26 of Chapter 1
20. See Note 13
21. Consumer Council. 1994. *Report on the Supermarket Industry in Hong Kong.* Hong Kong
22. Consumer Council. 1997. *The Practice of Resale Price Maintenance in Hong Kong.* Hong Kong
23. The Environment, Transport & Works Bureau, the HKSAR government. January 2006. Legislative Council brief. Hong Kong
24. Transport International Holdings website (www.tih.hk)
25. Civic Exchange. November 2009. *Paying for a Cleaner Bus Fleet.* Hong Kong

Chapter 4 : Land and Competition

1. See Note 43 of Chapter 1
2. Yuming Fu and Stephen Ching. 2001. *Examining Competition in Land Market: An Application of Event Study to Land Auctions in Hong Kong.* Madison: University of Wisconsin-Madison
3. Loh, Christine and Citizens Party. 1997. *The Government's High Land Price Policy: Can Hong Kong People Afford It?* Hong Kong
4. Hong Kong Democratic Foundation. 1999. *HKDF Newsltter No. 12: Government's Role in the Economy.* Hong Kong
5. See Note 17 of Chapter 1
6. Consumer Council . 1996. *Competition Policy: The Key to Hong Kong's Future Economic Success.* Hong Kong
7. Trade and Industry Bureau , the HKSAR Government. 1997. *Government's Response to the Consumer Council's Report on Competition Policy.* Hong Kong
8. Competition Policy Advisory Group. 1998. *Statement on Competition Policy.* Hong Kong
9. Webb, David (www.webb-site.com). 2001. *Hong Kong Needs a Competition Law*

Chapter 5 : Social and Economic Ills

1. Hong Kong Housing Authority website (http://www.housingauthority.gov.hk)
2. *Fortune.* May 2, 2002. *Who Needs Hong Kong?*
3. *Hong Kong Property Review.* January 2003. Hong Kong
4. Reis Inc's website (www.reis.com)
5. Business Week Online Asia (www.businessweek.com/asia/). December 18, 2000. *Warnings for Hong Kong in an Online Retailer's Demise*
6. Asia Times Online (www.atimes.com). July 10, 2002. *Hong Kong's Unkind Cut*
7. Hong Kong Confederation of Trade Unions (HKCTU). 2002. *Annual Survey of Violations of Trade Union Rights.* Hong Kong
8. World Socialist Website (www.wsws.org). July 8, 2000. *Opposition Grows in Hong Kong to Beijing's Big Business Administration*
9. CNN website (www.cnn.com). June 26, 2002. *The Inevitable Decline of Hong Kong and the Clash of Civilizations*
10. Asiaweek (www.asiaweek.com). November 27, 1998
11. See Legislative Council website. "Penny Stock Incident – Database on Particular Policy Issues" (http://www.legco.gov.hk/database/english/data_fa/fa-penny-stocks.htm)
12. The Expert Group to Review the Operation of the Securities and Futures Market Regulatory Structure. March 21, 2003. Report. Hong Kong
13. Webb, David (www.webb-site.com). 2003. *Disserving the Public Interest*

Chapter 6 : Possible Solutions

1. Citizens Party. 2001. *A New Direction for Public Housing in Hong Kong.* Hong Kong
2. Mexico government. 2002. Submission Paper to the APEC Competition Policy and Deregulation Workshop in Merida, Mexico, *The Role of Competition Policy in Economic Development.* Mexico
3. United Nations Conference on Trade and Development Secretariat. 2001. *Notes of Expert Meeting on Consumer Protection, Competition, Competitiveness and Development.*
4. United Nations Conference on Trade and Development Secretariat. 2002. *Report on Analysis of Market Access Issues Facing Developing Countries*
5. European Union. *Citizen's Guide to Competition Policy – Introduction*
6. European Union. *Citizen's Guide to Competition Policy – Liberalisation*
7. *YES Magazine.* Winter 2002. *Women, Citizenship, and the End of Poverty.* Helsinki
8. *Boston Review.* February/March 1996. *Time for a Wealth Tax?* Boston
9. Common Ground (USA). *The Key to Promoting Prosperity by Reducing Taxes on Labor and Capital*
10. Common Ground (USA). *An Open Letter to the Mayors of the Cities and Towns in the United States*
11. Land Value Taxation Campaign. *What is Land Value Taxation?*

Index